The Singer's Life
GOALS & ROLES

Stephen —
Best wishes for a successful personal and professional life as an <u>integral</u> singer!
Cliff Ware
August 27, 2008

The Singer's Life
GOALS & ROLES

CLIFTON WARE
University of Minnesota

Birch Grove Publishing

The Singer's Life: Goals and Roles

Copyright © 2005 Birch Grove Publishing. All rights reserved. Except as permitted under the United States Copyright Act of 1976, no part of this publication may be reproduced in any form or by any means, or stored in a data base or retrieval system, without the prior written permission of the publisher. Write to: Permissions, Birch Grove Publishing, P.O. Box 131327, Roseville, MN 55113.

Sponsoring Editor: Paul Nockleby
Manuscript Editor: Allison Bowman
Cover Design: Dawn Mathers Design

Library of Congress Cataloging-in-Publication Data

Ware, Clifton
    The Singer's Life: Goals and Roles/Clifton Ware
    x; 258 pp. 2 cm.
    Includes bibliographical references and index.
    ISBN 0-9744071-1-9
    1. Singing-Methods   I. Title
MT825.W18   2005

Manufactured in the U.S.A.
1 2 3 4 5 6 7 8 9 10 11 12 13 14 15 16

Contents

Preface/Acknowledgements

I ESTABLISHING MIND/BODY FOUNDATIONS
1. The Singer as Philosopher — 3
2. The Singer as Psychologist — 21
3. The Singer as Reconciler of Opposites — 35
4. The Singer as Vocal Athlete — 45
5. The Singer as Aural Processor — 57

II DEVELOPING AND EXECUTING VOCAL MUSIC SKILLS
6. The Singer as Musician — 71
7. The Singer as Vocal Technician — 81
8. The Singer as Linguist — 97
9. The Singer as Scholar — 107
10. The Singer as Communicator — 117

III EXPLORING AND ENHANCING CAREER OBJECTIVES
11. The Singer as Amateur or Professional — 133
12. The Singer as Business Manager — 147
13. The Singer as Pedagogue — 157
14. The Singer as Vocologist — 165
15. The Singer as Colleague — 177

IV SERVING SELF AND OTHERS
16. The Singer as Collaborator — 189
17. The Singer as Healer — 197
18. The Singer as Caregiver — 205
19. The Singer as Citizen — 219
20. The Singer as Achiever — 231

Bibliography — 243
Index — 251

Preface

The Singer's Life: Goals and Roles is based on a series of essays written for the National Opera Association's *Opera Journal*, as a five-year ongoing column titled "High Notes". In 1998 president Arvid Knudsen approached me about writing a brief quarterly column for NOA's *Opera Journal* on a topic of interest to singers. At that time, having been a singer for fifty years and a voice teacher for forty years, I thought I might have some worthwhile information to share with vocal musicians, so I enthusiastically accepted the assignment.

After giving serious consideration to potential topics, I settled on the idea of exploring the wide variety of roles played by singers (metaphorically speaking, the various hats worn by singers), both as vocal musicians and as human beings. So this series of essays focuses on the many complex challenges inherent in the voice profession, primarily from the point of view of classically trained singers, but also relevant to singers of non-classical music. To add a personal touch, throughout the book I've included some relevant anecdotes and experiences that relate to each role, as played out over my long career, beginning as a starry-eyed young singer and culminating as a teacher, mentor, and writer.

Although the original order of *Opera Journal* topics was presented somewhat randomly, they have been rearranged into a logical sequence more suitable for a book format. As the table of contents illustrates, the first section begins with the foundations of singing, progresses in the second section to vocal music skills, addresses career objectives in section three, and culminates in the fourth section with topics focusing on humanitarian service and legacy. Thus, in the first half we consider mind-body preparations for a vocal music career, followed by an overview of basic vocal music skills and ways to develop them. In the second half we look at ways to explore and develop sustainable vocal careers, and we conclude by discussing roles involving human relationships and responsibilities as we strive to fulfill personal life goals.

We human beings have many roles to play, but our mastery of the requisite skills to excel in any single area may vary widely, from favored areas that are strong, to neglected areas that are weak. For example, we all know singers who are very successful professionally but have unstable personal lives. Conversely, we also know singers who enjoy rich personal lives, yet are relatively unsuccessful in their vocal music careers. Then there's the singer with a gorgeous vocal instrument, but who is deficient in musical, linguistic, or dramatic skills. Or the singer who is highly motivated, organized, and industrious, but lacks people skills. Though it's not easy being all things to all people, singers are challenged to fulfill all latent potentialities in becoming integrated, well-rounded persons.

Of course, the connections between roles are often blurred, with considerable overlapping, as happens between such compatible roles as husband and father, or lover and friend. Yet, by looking at the individual roles we play in greater detail, we may more clearly understand and appreciate the many facets of our humanity, within a contextual framework that encompasses the whole person each of us desires to be. After all, is it really possible — or, more to the point, healthy — to separate our personal lives from our professional lives? Isn't the ultimate human goal to develop a balanced life, whereby both life areas and all roles mutually enhance and reinforce one another in positive ways? As you rightly discern, the answer to the first question is "no", and to the second question, "yes".

As you read this book, I hope you gain sufficient information that will help you understand and appreciate the many goals and roles that need to be mastered in your lifelong quest to become a well-rounded vocal musician and human being. Finally, I welcome your queries, suggestions, corrections, and comments. Please feel free to contact me (warex001@umn.edu).

ACKNOWLEDGEMENTS

At the outset I gratefully acknowledge the persuasive influence of my agent and editor, Paul Nockleby, whose persistent professional prodding and guidance led me to write this book. If it hadn't been for Paul's encouragement, I'd probably never have produced my first two books — *Adventures in Singing* (first edition, 1995) and *Basics of Vocal Pedagogy* (1998), both published by McGraw-Hill. Prior to meeting Paul, my wife, Bettye, and I enjoyed five years of limited success in self-publishing and promoting our publication, *Voice Adventures*, so it took some gentle persuasion to let him undertake initiatives on our behalf. True to form, with this book Paul provided invaluable editorial comments and suggestions, and we are very grateful for his expert assistance.

I'm forever indebted to my musical partner and wife, Bettye, for her patience and long-suffering support of my many special projects. She willingly reads most of my materials, offering her constructive opinions and editorial advice. Whenever her approval is granted on any project, I can rest assured it's OK to proceed. I'm very fortunate to have a wife who not only is a superb musician, but also has a MA degree in English literature.

Also, my deepest appreciation goes to the National Opera Association's former president, Arvid Knudsen, who originally invited me to write an ongoing column titled "High Notes", the articles of which form the content of this book. Thanks, too, to Robert Thieme, editor of the *Opera Journal* for his editorial collaboration and for granting me permission to use these previously published articles for this book.

There are so many other persons who have had major influences on my singing, including choral directors, voice teachers, and other teachers with whom I've studied, fellow colleagues and co-workers with whom I've collaborated, numbers of students who have helped me develop my teaching skills, and co-workers, friends, and relatives who have supported my talents and goals. Without an extensive network of professional and personal associations I would not have gained the broad background of experience needed to write this book. I'm happy to express my sincerest appreciation to all who have played various roles in my life.

In this book I faithfully try to cover most aspects of the singer's life, including all major goals and roles. If any significant topics or concerns are overlooked, I would appreciate hearing about them. There's a possibility that a future edition will include new contributions from readers, so please let me hear from you.

Part I
Establishing Mind/Body Foundations

Chapter 1

The Singer as Philosopher

Philosophy, briefly defined as the love or pursuit of wisdom, is often depicted as a search for profound answers. But philosophy also guides practical life, for example in choice of career, how we interpret a given song text, and the total personal artistry that we bring to each vocal performance.

In this chapter ten guidelines summarize my philosophy of singing. These guidelines flow from many sources, and are elaborated throughout the rest of the book.

1. Understand Your Potential for Expressive Communication

The human voice, justly considered by some as the king or queen of instruments, provides an unequalled vehicle for expression, primarily because thoughts and feelings are communicated through words and sounds emanating from a place deep within each of us. Most humans, regardless of race, ethnicity or social standing, are endowed with vocal mechanisms that permit a higher level of functioning than is typically realized. But many singers do not function at an optimal level due to differences in talent, motivation, time, effort and education. Though we are wired and programmed to sing with efficiency and expression, there is much to learn about the "vocal mystery" that has not been sufficiently explored nor explained.

The larynx first evolved about 300 million years ago in fish, then progressed to mammals via amphibians, and then to humans. The purposes of the primitive larynx were to keep foreign matter out of the lungs, to assist elimination of body wastes, and to help compress air for lifting. As the larynx evolved, it descended in the throat to a lower level than in other primates, thereby creating human potential for vocal communication that gradually evolved into heightened expression.

The higher level of expression evidenced by humans — in comparison with other primates — is attributed to a more highly developed brain and neural system that has evolved to meet increasing demands of survival, including the increased need to communicate more clearly, expansively, and subtly. Thus the unique configuration of the human vocal apparatus (torso, breathing system, larynx, and vocal tract) has evolved to create an optimal sound-producing mechanism. Humans are uniquely wired and programmed to sing.

2. Sing and Enjoy a Challenging Self-Improvement Program

As a young singer, I made a mind-expanding discovery during my undergraduate years, at a time when I was seeking my life's mission. Having started out as a voice major, after two years I switched to philosophy. Why? Primarily because singing began to appear frivolous, irrelevant to the type of life work a serious adult should pursue. My impression was that truly significant occupations were in medicine, law, architecture, and scientific research. So for two years I sought answers to life's questions by studying philosophy, eventually reaching one unsettling conclusion: there are no satisfactory answers — only more questions!

The final eye-opener came when discussing career choices with my principal philosophy professor, who advised me to complete my music major because I was adept at singing and enjoyed it. Looking back at that moment, I am grateful that I was encouraged to pursue what I have since come to view as one of the most challenging, relevant, and integrative life-long occupations a person can pursue.

Indeed, I maintain that singing provides the greatest self-improvement course one can undertake. The virtues of vocal study are well substantiated and summarized in a handout published by the American Academy of Teachers of Singing in New York City. According to the handout, "Singing fortifies health, widens culture, refines the intelligence, enriches the imagination, makes for happiness and endows life with an added zest." In addition, twelve specific reasons are listed:

Singing

- is healthful; it develops the lungs and purifies the blood by emptying more completely the lungs of used air and filling them deeply with fresh air.

- promotes good posture and graceful carriage.

- lends expressiveness to the countenance and animation to the mind.

- increases poise and self-confidence, and develops character through difficulties overcome.

- gives a pleasanter, richer speaking voice and improved speech, thereby adding to the charm of personality.

- strengthens memory and concentration.

- acquaints one with the inner meaning of words, and

thus stimulates deeper insight into poetry and prose.

• enables one to understand and enjoy more fully the art of great singers.

• awakens interest in the beauties of music and admits one to the rich and varied treasury of the literature of song.

• brings new aspirations and new buoyancy to life through the absorbing pursuit of an ideal.

• as a means of self-expression is a medium of release for pent-up emotions.

• though followed with no thought of professionalism, gives pleasure to one's self and ultimately to one's friends. Its appeal is universal.

3. Develop a Positive Attitude To Achieve Optimal Results

Expressive singing requires a constant supply of positive thoughts, constructive self-talk, and creative interpretation of distracting, demanding, or difficult external conditions to elicit appropriate neuro-muscular responses. The goal for the singer is to project a confident, outgoing stage persona while remaining sufficiently vulnerable to allow a wide range of emotions to be communicated through vocal, musical, and dramatic means.

In his landmark study, *Emotion and Adaptation* (1991), the cognitive psychologist Richard S. Lazarus identifies as "goal congruent" the positive emotions of happiness/joy, pride, love/affection, and relief. Lazarus identifies as negative and "goal incongruent" the emotions of anger, fright/anxiety, guilt/shame, sadness, envy/jealousy, and disgust. (See Chapter 2, and especially "Responses to Stress" on pp. 26-27.)

We know from teaching and mentoring hundreds of singers that those who model *positive attitudes* are more likely to achieve their goals than those who hold negative attitudes. Because negative emotions (anger, fear, shame, sadness, etc.) are transmitted subconsciously, our overall attitude affects our spirit and therefore our attractiveness to others. A positive outlook (a "half-full cup" attitude) is always more beneficial and productive than a "half-empty cup" attitude.

Since right thinking leads to right action, ridding the mind of mental tensions is the first step in creating conditions for effective vocal performance. Thus, when we singers encounter a frustrating person or problem (such as criticism from a colleague or difficulty learning a song) a positive, can-do attitude propels us toward our vision while resentment and anger sidetrack us and divert energy from our goal.

To communicate the entire spectrum of positive emotions, the singer-actor must be willing to let go of inhibitions. Such vulnerability requires a risk-tolerant, secure, outgoing, optimistic personality. A charismatic, enthusiastic singer has a deeply-felt passion for singing and desires above all to inspire this same emotion in others.

4. Embrace Learning and Change

Though a singer spends much time alone researching, studying and practicing, a large part of learning to sing is communal, requiring the feedback, participation, and guidance of others. The learning process is ongoing, and involves continuous adjustments in our belief systems and behavior. If we aren't learning, we stagnate.

Ironically, when it comes to vocal production or self-identity, some singers refuse to make changes suggested by instructors. Ideally, a singer is never defensive when receiving instruction, but open-minded and receptive to constructive input or feedback.

The American philosopher John Dewey cautioned against fearing or passively acquiescing to inevitable changes in situations, conditions, and events. Instead, he recommended utilizing and directing all changes in fulfilling our objectives Throughout my career I've faced various types of situations that have required learning new behaviors, including changing career paths and developing a more efficient vocal production. Yet, more than five decades after my advisor suggested switching from philosophy to vocal performance (leading me to explore various aspects of singing and teaching), I maintain my philosophical roots by distilling what I have learned in writings.

5. Develop An Authentic Voice Using Efficient Vocal Technique

The singer's primary goal is to discover the authentic voice within — what Cornelius Reid has termed a natural "vocal ecology" — which avoids copycat techniques and commercial influences, and allows the vocal instrument to be used in a healthy, efficient, and expressive manner throughout one's lifespan. Thus, our philosophical quest must lead to discovering the most effective way to sing or speak. For instance, do we sing the way we are equipped by nature to sing — based on inherited mind-body characteristics, with an honest intent to maximize the capacity of our vocal mechanisms — or do we adjust our vocal productions to suit the ideals of others?

Perhaps no vocal topic is more controversial than the question of which vocal productions and styles are most suitable for communication and expression. While the elite position of art-music favors classical traditions, the general public prefers popular styles. Classical traditions have remained relatively stable for several hundred years (the twentieth century was an exceptional period of increasing experimentation). Meanwhile, popular music trends have varied greatly over the past several decades, hastened by an explosion of new forms and the advent of digital sound recording and broadcasting. Between classical and popular music forms, there are a multitude of folk traditions, many of which are embraced in various ways by both classical and popular genres. Numerous examples of hybrid vocal music forms encapsulate the best qualities of classical, pop, and folk genres, prominent among them such works as Leonard Bernstein's masterpiece musical *West Side Story*.

Most vocal authorities agree that, regardless of the type of music a singer performs, the important thing is singing efficiently, with solid technique. For this reason, many singers learn to sing using classical vocal music rather than pop, primarily because classical music is based on an athletic, energetic, and efficient vocal production that facilitates the development of an extended vocal range, increased dynamic levels, greater sustaining power, and wider range of expressive means. In terms of artistic challenges, classical vocal music is characterized by attention to detail and variety of expression, textual and musical intricacies, specifically defined styles, an extensive range of harmonic treatment, and a more profound meaning that requires subtle interpretative nuances.

On the other hand, pop music and folk music are associated with less complicated forms and simpler content, though it's true that some forms of pop music are just as challenging as classical vocal music. Then, too, there are some pop and folk songs that provide excellent learning vehicles for young singers and encourage efficient vocalism. To illustrate the comparative challenges found in the two genres, compare the simplicity of the popular song "Happy Birthday" to the complexity and substance of an art song such as Franz Schubert's "Gretchen am Spinnrade." Practically anyone can sing the former, while only a well-trained singer can render the Schubert song effectively. In any case, whether pop, folk or classical, the ultimate test for any composition is its ability to continue communicating over generations and centuries, based on inherent characteristics that reflect the essential principles upon which all lasting artworks are created.

The classical vocal model follows the rules of voice production taught in the vocal art of Western Civilization, chiefly as developed over the centuries through the *bel canto* ("beautiful singing") vocal tradition. The *bel canto* style first originated in Italian polyphonic (multi-part) and courtly solo singing of the late sixteenth century, and was further developed in Italian opera in the seventeenth through early nineteenth centuries. Though approaches to singing have varied, with other prominent schools developing in Germany, England, and France, the predominant classical vocal method is based on the traditional Italian *bel canto* approach. As renowned vocal pedagogue Richard Miller has stated in his book — *The Structure of Singing: System and Art in Vocal Technique*:

> Vocal timbre that results from the well-formed, well-coordinated instrument, without maladjustment of any of its physical parts or functions, stands the best chance of qualifying under the artistic creation for tonal beauty, as found in Western culture. (Miller 1986, p. 205)

According to classical definitions from ancient Greek philosophy, the characteristics required for an object to be considered beautiful are *unity, contrast, proportion*, and *balance*. A sculpture depicting a human body is classical when physical features are neither understated nor exaggerated. Other art objects, including songs, must adhere to these four principles to be considered "classical".

There are many ways of producing vocal tone, as witnessed by the variety of singers performing in numerous pop and classical styles. However, if our philosophy of singing involves maintaining long-term healthy voice use and developing a wide range of expressive means, we must sing efficiently. And, in the process of developing a dependable vocal technique, we will discover our authentic voices. This mission is achieved by developing self-knowledge, a life-long process involving an honest assessment of our values, desires, weaknesses and strengths, level of innate talent, and motivation to succeed.

6. Choose Your Vocal Icons and Voice Production Wisely

Most vocal problems heard today, both in classical and pop singing, are the direct result of singers imitating their vocal icons, either consciously or unconsciously. As expected, the unfortunate result is a growing legacy of singing practices based on imitation or pseudo vocalism. Some of the mimicked singers on the pop side include country twangers, pop crooners, gospel belters, and hard-rock blasters. And on the classical side we have choral hooters, wobbly warblers, tense-tongued tenors, and dark-throated basses.

As mentioned earlier, our goal as singers is to discover and develop our authentic voices rather than copying others. Understandably, until a belief and behavior system is completely our own, it cannot be truly effective. This is not to say that one should not adopt others' beliefs, but only to emphasize the importance of claiming such beliefs and behaviors as one's own. Hence, though we may admire the vocal production of certain icons (who may actually serve as appropriate models), we should avoid imitation and strive to discover our true voices.

To address this issue, I've made a recording that illustrates many of these voices. I've learned through trial and error how to produce a variety of voice productions, with the added good fortune of eventually having discovered what I deem to be my authentic voice. The CD — *Vocal Explorations: The Bad, the Good, and the "Other"* — was a culmination of a search for a dependable singing technique. I've spent many years exploring various types of vocal productions, and I've recently used mimicking techniques in teaching voice production, primarily to show that we are capable of using our voices in many ways.

On the CD, I discuss five principles that guide my approach to singing technique:

1. The primary goal of learning to sing is to actualize one's authentic, natural vocal potential, rather than to imitate someone else.

2. The act of singing is based on a simple process, which is complicated by psycho-emotional, social, and physical influences that make it difficult to master optimal vocal technique.

3. Most singers never achieve their full technical and artistic potential, ostensibly because it is easier to settle into a "comfort zone" created by the positive reinforcement of well-meaning admirers.

4. Many singers, both classical and non-classical, are content with using a mimicking approach based on

the vocal, stylistic, and interpretive mannerisms of well-known model singers.

5. The ability to mimic various voice productions and styles may provide a useful technique for discerning vocal mannerisms, effectively sharpening one's senses and raising awareness of cause/effect relationships (for example, when tongue tension creates a restricted vocal tone, or a relaxed tongue results in a freer tone).

We are all confronted with hard choices concerning the type of vocalism we will use to express our thoughts and emotions. That's where a voice teacher comes in. In order to identify and express our genuine, potential selves, we must strive to realize our authentic voices by optimizing our vocal production in speaking and singing. We are very lucky if we have an instructor who can help us find and use our true voice.

For inexplicable reasons, in singing it's perfectly acceptable to use the vocal instrument in an inefficient manner, but inefficient use of the body by an athlete would never be acceptable behavior in competitive sports. No one would ever consider intentionally handicapping football players using physical maladjustments, applying splints on joints to reduce movement, heavy weights around the ankles and wrists to prevent speed and dexterity, blindfolds and ear plugs to limit seeing and hearing, and so on.

Yet singers often willingly handicap themselves by using manipulative voice productions that inhibit tone, dynamics, and range, and even worse threaten vocal longevity. Why do singers willingly make such damaging choices? Primarily because they wish to cater to the whims of fans craving "let it all hang out" performances that elicit obvious negative physical and vocal tensions. One of the saddest commentaries on our contemporary culture is that some forms of popular music actually consider aberrant vocal behavior as a normal form of vocal expression. The answer to such vocal mayhem is striving to maximize the full potential of our instrument. Such a noble pursuit requires applying constructive techniques that allow us to release the "authentic voice" within us, not a manipulated, distorted, imitative facsimile of personally selected "model" singers.

In both classical and popular music styles, including folk traditions, the voice is often manipulated to achieve expressive effects. Why does the singing of so many world cultures, especially primitive ones, evidence pressed or stressed vocal production? Daily life in primitive societies, it seems, creates a natural tension that is inevitably expressed in voice production. In turn, this high level of tension is promoted through learned imitative behavior. Even in contemporary times, the angst of certain popular singers, notably hard-rockers, is often marked by vocal stress and distortion, the result of muscular tensions created in the vocal tract, particularly in muscles of the articulating organs, neck, and throat, but also including muscles of the torso and respiratory system.

Maria Callas, an icon among opera aficionados, is an example of an artist who ruined her voice, possibly through a combination of health problems, wide-ranging repertoire, and questionable artistic choices. Sadly, Callas' voice showed a steady decline throughout her career, from exceptional coloratura in the early stages to a severely challenged mezzo-soprano title role in the opera *Carmen* near the end.

Though touted as an exemplary singing actress, Maria Callas' downfall was probably the result of allowing emotions and histrionics to supersede her attention to vocal production, which in turn forced her to rely on more emotion and histrionics to get through her dramatic roles. Sadly, her fans may have hastened her eventual demise.

7. Coordinate Your Voice to Achieve the "Golden Mean"

Learning to reconcile opposites in singing is essential. Consider, for instance, the challenge of reconciling relaxation with tension, a particularly difficult task because muscles work in opposites; one set activating (agonists) while the opposing set (antagonists) relaxes. This process, known as *muscular antagonism*, forms the basis for all muscle activity.

Coordination of the entire vocal process includes volition, respiration, phonation, resonation, and articulation. Balanced phonation is characterized by a vocal-fold closure that is neither tight nor loose, and results in a flowing tone that rides on the breath. When resonation and phonation conditions are maximized, the harmonic spectrum is balanced between highs and lows, and the coordinated result is *chiaroscuro*, the "bright-dark" tone prized by Italian vocal pedagogues. When a singer's registers are coordinated, there is a seamless blend from top to bottom, with no bumps, cracks, or changes in tonal quality.

All of the above are discussed more thoroughly in other chapters, particularly Chapter 3, which deals with the reconciliation of opposites, and Chapter 7, which concentrates on vocal technique.

8. Perform With Artistry To Achieve Effective Communication

As singers, we must remember that the ultimate goal is to effectively communicate the message of a composition to an audience, according to the creative intent of the composer and textual source. The combined vocal, musical and dramatic conveyance of ideas, thoughts, emotions, and stories are filtered through a singer's unique viewpoint, talents, and abilities.

Understanding of a composition demands a well-balanced individual who uses systematic thought processes to analyze and explore all dimensions of the music and text. Soulful, deeply felt interpretations emerge from singers who are sensitive to others, curious about all aspects of life, and willing to ferret out the meaning of a vocal composition.

Communication is also dependent upon the persona we develop and project, a reflection of how we feel about our work and ourselves. Every singer must pay careful attention to the way he or she is perceived by others, including physical carriage, dress, grooming, and demeanor. A singer lacking in self-confidence and charisma is severely handicapped in performance.

The ability to see oneself objectively is crucial in developing a commanding stage presence. Audio and video recordings allow singers to see themselves objectively, as well as to assess their performance skills from the standpoint of outside observers.

9. Create a Game Plan, from Short-Range to Long-Range Goals

Achieving the loftiest goal begins with a first step. I recommend writing a mission statement summarizing in a single paragraph what you wish to accomplish, in conjunction with a game plan based on short, medium, and long-range objectives. It's important to revise this mission statement periodically as you continue developing your vocal music talent.

Although my goals have undergone many changes, I've

remained focused on my life's mission. I started out as a child visual artist, developed into a singer during high school, and in college majored first in philosophy, then music. My musical career took a winding path, including service as a church musician, choir director, and part-time professional singer. Since beginning my university-level teaching career, I've held positions as voice teacher, choral director, opera director, and pedagogy instructor. Throughout my entire career I've served as a mid-level administrator, and, in recent years, I've written vocal music textbooks. So, who says we can't reinvent ourselves along life's journey, changing our goals as we continue to learn and grow?

The second step, after writing a mission statement, is to order priorities according to importance. By prioritizing your objectives, you will be guided in committing the time and effort needed to achieve the goals you deem most important. List and rank your top priorities, and reassess your goals periodically. Ask yourself if some conditions in your life have changed, such as marriage, job, or health. If so, perhaps it's time for reassessment. Wishy-washy commitments will prove frustrating, but it's good to be flexible in setting goals and making plans.

Third, begin each day with a clear understanding of your desired goals and objectives. Organize and manage time and events around these personal priorities. As each objective is completed, check it off your list, and, if it is not completed, carry it forward for a future date. Scratching off tasks when completed provides a sense of accomplishment.

10. Work Consistently and Trust the Process

No matter how talented a singer may be, there's always room for improvement, at any level. Singers who think they can afford to take it easy may find themselves sitting on the sidelines wondering what happened. This is not to imply that singers should refrain from taking breaks, vacations, or time off to retool, but rather to warn against complacency, laziness, and overconfidence. The need to stay engaged as a lifelong learner cannot be overemphasized. The most successful singers are committed to achieving excellence, not only as singers but as human beings. Model singers balance their professional and personal lives, understanding that the two are mutually reinforcing.

By applying oneself consistently in mastering the many skills associated with singing — vocal, musical, dramatic, linguistic, business matters, etc. — positive growth will occur. Every singer experiences setbacks along the way, some resulting in discouragement, disappointment, despair, and depression. In such situations, however, your philosophy of singing (that is, why you have chosen it as a serious pursuit) should lift your spirits.

There will be plateaus of learning and achievement, when progress seems stymied — though in reality some undetected learning is occurring. In such cases, my advice is to stay the course, trust the learning process, and have patience that it will eventually lead to some positive breakthrough.

Of course, faith without work will be fruitless, so it is imperative that you remain committed to doing what it takes to improve. If you are diligent, keep the faith that good things can happen to you. As Alexander Pope so poignantly stated:

> *Hope springs eternal in the human breast,*
> *Man never is, but always to be blest.*

Notable Quotes: The Singer as Philosopher

What role do the arts play in society?

> Arts education is no less valuable as a collective training than school sports. It's just as important to explore the imagination through literature, poetry, and song as it is to develop young bodies, and develop attitudes of teamwork and a team mentality through sports. But the real bottom line is that every major genius personality in the 20th century — even dear Stephen Hawking, who wasn't always terrifically handicapped in his life — has been a romantic, liberal arts-dedicated, renaissance-thinking person. Einstein's letters contain some of the most beautiful thoughts, not only on the intimate details of his very fascinating personal life, but also on the importance of humanity, great imagination — and that the only thing limiting us is how we limit ourselves . . . We are now coming to a search for depth and context, a sort of "where's the meat" attitude, that is splashing into the arts, and is certainly splashing into American music. I think we're on the brink of some really interesting developments. — Thomas Hampson

What can we learn from history to inform us about the current role of music in society?

> I feel that we have a responsibility to understand those that have been here before us. We're not experiencing anything new — the paradigm is different; the context is different, the tools are perhaps different — but the motivation is still there . . . This is something Joseph Campbell was treating. All of these things find a tremendous fruition in music and literature . . . And I think all of these huge things that

we are talking about, are in fact, endemic to song in its final form. And that's what poetry is . . . and music is the context in which that dialogue and that manipulation of poetic context become so fascinating. Nothing, as far as I'm concerned, lives in isolation.
— Thomas Hampson

Chapter 2

The Singer as Psychologist

Why Gain Psychological Insight?

As a singer for more than 50 years, I've discovered, dealt with, and mostly overcome my own entanglements (or "hang-ups"). I experienced joy as a young person when I first discovered I had an above-average vocal talent and was able to exploit it fully. After the thrill of singing evolved into a professional "ought to sing" perspective, expectations of perfection were soon thrown in. Vocal problems then resulted from a strong drive to succeed as a singer and a tendency to push too hard. For instance, my back muscles would ache following a recital, undoubtedly due to muscle tensions. Later, I was able to develop a more efficient vocal technique that better reflected my innate vocal character. Now that I can accomplish what I would like to have achieved at the beginning, singing can still be stressful, especially if a lot of memory work is involved.

Everyone in vocal music is familiar with singers suffering from common hang-ups that directly affect their vocal development, resulting in minimal if any progress. The more obvious difficulties are: learning disabilities, such as dyslexia and attention deficit disorder (ADD); psycho-emotional disorders, notably panic attacks and perfectionism; and vocal-identity issues, such as identifying the self too closely with one's voice.

Other psycho-emotional hang-ups can be discerned through close observation of a singer's behavior. Muscular and skeletal arrangements on stage, for example, tend to reflect a singer's sense of security, self-esteem, and even overall psychological adjustment to life events and circumstances. "He looks tied up in knots" or "She's completely uninvolved and boring" are common assessments of a singer's body language. "Nervous tic" physical mannerisms such as fidgeting, scratching, blinking, twitching or trembling, are symptoms of insecurity; while the tendency to armor oneself self-protectively creates physical tensions that inhibit natural vocalism and expression, a common defense mechanism nearly every singer must overcome.

Hang-ups may be rooted in adolescence when newly-minted adult male and female voices cause periods of instability and insecurity. Singers in their 20s are sometimes still wrestling with adolescent issues, including self-esteem and acceptance of their natural voice type. The most anxious period developmentally is between ages 25 and 35, when performance careers are often made or broken. The decade following the peak years — approximately ages 25-35 — is also a very anxious period for some singers. Later, as age creeps up, and along with it the loss of vocal powers and professional viability, new hang-ups may occur.

Developing Self Awareness

Socrates' injunction — "Know thyself' — is worthwhile advice for singers of any age. His exhortation to rigorous self-examination can be subdivided into seven goals:

- to perceive reality (life events and activities) accurately, so as to distinguish realistic probabilities from one-in-a-million (win-the-lottery) possibilities;

- to reconcile who we are with the person we dream to be, so as to maximize the chance that we will fulfill our true potential;

- to acquire and develop the knowledge, skills, and strategies for reaching our realistic goals and objectives;

- to accept ambiguity and paradox, and to reconcile personality/voice, mind/body, being/doing, process/ends, and technique/artistry in unified, constructive behaviors;

- to interact with the outside world in a life-affirming manner — physically, emotionally, and socially;

- to communicate with and relate to other persons at the highest possible level of creative expression; and

- to achieve a state of purpose and connection, to the point that we see who we are in history, culture, and society.

To achieve all of the above is to arrive at a state of grace, or what some call "bliss".

The goal of the singer as psychologist is not just to fix our hang-ups. As Martin Seligman, the founder of Positive Psychology, puts it,

> Psychology is not just the study of disease, weakness, and damage; it also is the study of strength and virtue. Treatment is not just fixing what is wrong; it also is building what is right. Psychology is not just about illness or health; it is about work, education, insight, love, growth, and play. And in this quest for what is best, Positive Psychology does not rely on wishful thinking, self-deception or hand waving; instead it tries to adapt what is best in the scientific

method to the unique problems that human behavior presents in all its complexity. (Seligman 2002)

Psychology, therefore, is the study of what makes us tick. We study it to help us self-actualize, to help us be the best we can be. Even so, we sometimes have no choice but to treat the "warts" in order to get smooth skin.

What psychological lessons can we draw from 50 years in this business? Above all, it is to spend the time and effort to get to know yourself thoroughly, including strengths and weaknesses. With 20/20 hindsight, I think I would have benefited from maintaining a journal of my goals and activities, with reflections on my accomplishments as well as how I was feeling about my singing life. If I could start over, I would pay more attention to my body's response to its environment as well as my thinking, feeling, and learning style. Such introspection would have involved learning new strategies, including yoga, Tai Chi, and the Alexander Technique (all of which are now highly recommended by voice professionals).

Motivation and Emotion

A singer's *motivation* provides energy, direction, and even passion for performing challenging vocal repertoire in an expressive manner. Strong motivation energizes and directs goal-oriented behavior in constructive ways. *Emotion*, on the other hand, is subjective awareness of motivation that also includes physiological arousal ("I love to sing, and enjoy the adrenaline rush that accompanies enthusiastic audience applause") due to a stimulus, either real or imagined. A singer's emotion is revealed in body language, facial expression, posture, and voice. Singers may also unwittingly communicate emotion through facial twitches, perspiration, shaking legs, fidgeting fingers, roving eyes, slumping posture, and lethargic vocalism.

Of course, every time a singer opens his or her mouth to perform, an emotion is involved. Whether the singer is performing a simple vocal exercise or an aria, the emotion may be distraction or fear on the negative side, or excitement or determination on the positive side.

Whatever the emotion, it affects the vocal production. Singers should therefore consciously adopt emotions that will elicit favorable responses. Of these, my favorite is the emotion of *joyous surprise*, as though one has just received wonderful news that creates excitement. This type of emotion sets up the appropriate mind-body conditions by relaxing the articulators (jaw, tongue, etc.) and throat muscles, thereby allowing a deeper, more relaxed breath; it also activates the appropriate muscle responses for singing, especially in the vocal tract and breathing system.

The Singer's Brain and Emotional Life

Brain-wave studies have shown that the two hemispheres of the brain are related in different ways to emotional processes. The right (dominant) hemisphere is more adept at discriminating negative emotions, while the left hemisphere is more involved in processing positive emotions. Voice function in the brain is associated with groups of neurons in a brain structure known as the *periaqueductal gray* (PAG) part of the emotional motor system. This primitive system allows animals to survive and thrive in a challenging and fast-paced environment.

Emotions are expressed and communicated through changes in the autonomic, somatic, and endocrine systems controlling heart rate, blood pressure, urination, sweating, breathing rate, facial expression, vocal production, body alignment, and gestures. The *fight or flight* syndrome is experienced by vocal performers who constantly cope with emotions and adrenaline flow when handling performance stress.

The fight-or-flight syndrome describes a person's response to normal social stress, with its physiological causes and effects. *Stress responses* may involve goal-directed actions to relieve symptoms, or defense (escape) mechanisms such as repression, denial, displacement, projection, regression, rationalization, intellectualization, or sublimation.

RESPONSES TO STRESS

Confrontive Coping
I stand my ground and fight for what I want
I try to get the person responsible to change his or her mind
I express anger to the person(s) who caused the problem
I let my feelings out somehow
I take a big chance or do something very risky
I do something that won't work, but at least I am doing something

Distancing
I make light of the situation; refuse to get too serious about it
I go on as if nothing has happened
I don't let it get to me; refuse to think too much about it
I try to forget the whole thing
I look for the silver lining; look on the bright side of things
I go along with fate; sometimes I just have bad luck

Self-Controlling
I try to keep my feelings to myself
I keep others from knowing how bad things are
I try not to burn my bridges, but leave things open somewhat
I try not to act too hastily or follow my first hunch
I keep my feelings from interfering with other things too much
I think about how a person I admire would handle this and use that as a guide
I try to see things from the other person's point of view

Seeking Social Support
I talk to someone to find out more about the situation
I talk to someone who can do something concrete about the problem
I ask a relative or friend I respect for advice
I talk to someone about how I am feeling
I accept sympathy and understanding from someone
I get professional help

Most singers are familiar with three common stress reduction strategies: confrontation, compromise, and withdrawal. Psychological studies, however, have shown that the most personally satisfying ways of coping with stress are *planful problem-solving* and *positive reappraisal* (see examples of these and other strategies in the chart below). In general,

---

Accepting Responsibility
    I criticize or lecture myself
    I realize I brought the problem on myself
    I promise myself that things will be different next time
    I apologize or do something to make up

Escape-Avoidance
    I wish that the situation would go away or be over with
    I hope a miracle will happen
    I have fantasies or wishes about how things might turn out
    I try to make myself feel better by eating, drinking, medication, smoking, etc.
    I avoid being with people in general
    I refuse to believe that it has happened
    I take it out on other people
    I sleep more than usual

Planful Problem-Solving [prospective]
    I know what has to be done, so I double my efforts to make things work
    I make a plan of action and follow it
    I just concentrate on what I have to do next
    I change something so things will turn out all right
    I draw on my past experiences; I was in a similar situation before
    I come up with a couple of different solutions to the problem

Positive Reappraisal [retrospective]
    I changed or grew as a person in a good way
    I came out of the experience better than when I went in
    I found new faith
    I rediscovered what is important in life
    I prayed
    I changed something about myself
    I was inspired to do something creative

From *The Ways of Coping CheckList* (Folkman & Lazarus, 1985)

these strategies include commitment to a goal, acceptance of challenge, a willingness to take calculated risks, and an optimistic attitude toward unacceptable outcomes (past), or less-than-ideal circumstances (present).

Finding and internalizing an appropriate emotional state for singing is a primary objective for all singers. For instance, the calm state, as evidenced by being satisfied, content, at peace, or relaxed (*let-go*), is a primary state upon which all other emotions can be layered during performance. Thus, rather than actually feeling and mimicking typical negative emotions in performance, one maintains a calm, grounded, focused state that allows the layering-on of imagined "idealized" emotions, without the typical muscle tensions that accompany them in real life. Achieving such an ideal performing state is extremely difficult, and requires ongoing, rigorous self-examination.

In addition to these conscious approaches to stress-management, *meditative practices* are recommended for achieving a heightened awareness that calms, focuses, and centers the self prior to performance. Meditative disciplines (such as yoga) slow the pulse, relax the breathing, and calm the mind with peaceful images and experiences.

The Types of Intelligence Needed by Singers

The ability to think and problem-solve requires *intelligence* — the capacity to perceive, understand, or learn in new or trying situations. Seven distinct types of intelligence have been described by Howard Gardner (1983): linguistic, musical, logical, mathematical, spatial, kinesthetic, and the personal intelligences of self-understanding and interpersonal skills. Daniel Goleman (1995), a proponent of *emotional intelligence*, has emphasized the importance of self-understanding and interpersonal skills. These various intelligences are unevenly distributed among singers.

Even though eccentric, aggressive, self-centered singers may achieve stardom through sheer talent and drive, remaining at the top requires a degree of emotional and social intelligence.

Developing Memory for Singing

Learning may be defined as a change in behavior due to experience, as opposed to changes caused by instinct, maturation, or temporary mind/body states. Learning involves *thinking* processes, the essential components of which are *images* and *concepts*, which are needed for managing categories of objects and experiences. Singers rely heavily on imagery to achieve high-level performance.

A major component of learning is *memory*, one of the most useful skills for vocal musicians to cultivate. Memory retention, which is processed at molecular and neural levels in the limbic system and temporal lobe of the cerebral cortex, is measured in three ways: recall, recognition, and relearning. Forgetting information may be attributed to:
physiological conditions (disuse);
psycho-emotional disorders (repression);
inhibitions (interference by later memories); or
cognitive factors, such as the absence of incidental cues learned at the time information was encoded.

Effective cueing devices include:
mnemonic strategies (such as "Every Good Boy Does Fine" for the lines e-g-b-d-f in a treble clef);
loci (associations with places, such as in a walk through a garden to recall words of a song text);
imagery (such as imagining singing in the shape of an arched form above the head); or
acronyms (such as the three "P's" of vocal success: Practice, Persistence, and Patience).

Short-term memory has limited capacity for storage, but can be extended through techniques such as "chunking" (breaking up song texts into verses or sections, or rehearsing material to be retained through repetition). In contrast, *long-term memory* has more capacity and is organized on the basis of networks of associations and schemata, or patterns used for organizing material. Developing effective memory techniques can be the best defense against stress brought on by the fear of forgetting a passage in the middle of a performance.

The Role of Attitudes

An attitude consists of three components: beliefs, emotions, and behaviors. *Attitudes* are more focused than *values*, and similar to *opinions*. For example, though classically trained singers generally value classical art song, individual singers may hold varying opinions about certain types of art song, such as preferring German lieder to French mélodie.

Singers who hold positive attitudes are more likely to achieve their goals than those who hold negative attitudes. We begin to take control of our attitudes when we realize that our perceptions and interpretations profoundly affect our behavior. An effort to control attitude may be framed by a positive outlook (the "half-full-cup" rather than "half-empty-cup" attitude). When a singer encounters a negative experience of any type, be it negative criticism from a colleague or difficulty in learning a song, his or her response to the problem will make a significant difference in future progress.

An example of a harmful attitude is the widely shared public image (stereotype) of the "opera singer" as an overweight Wagnerian soprano. Whether we allow that image to take root in us, and to shape or distort our self-image or the image we have of others, is a measure of our emotional security and maturity. (See how soprano Deborah Voigt coped with this issue, pp. 54-55.)

Social Influence and Interaction

Social behavior is the province of social psychology, including social influence and interaction. *Social conformity* is the result of group pressure. Subjects tend to conform in matters of fact as well as of opinion, as evidenced by the way successful singers abide by the various social, musical, and artistic standards of the vocal profession. Obedience to authority varies, depending on the distance between the human subject and the authority figure (for example, singer and conductor), and the authority figure's legitimacy and respectability.

The basic processes of social interaction can be explained in terms of interpersonal relationships, group processes, and pro-social behavior. The first of these, interpersonal relationships, can be distinguished into three different types according to motivation:

affiliation, motivated by social comparison or desire to reduce fear;
friendship, which involves shifting from interpersonal attraction to valuing communality of interaction and personal investment; and
intimate relationships, based on liking or loving, compassion or passion, communication, and equality.

Group processes involve three or more people who interact with and influence each other, and include such group dynamics as *group polarization* (enhancing group opinion), *group-think* (granting a higher priority to cohesiveness than to quality of work), and *minority influence* (disagreeing using confidence, consistency, and persuasion).

Social behaviors such as reciprocity and responsibility encourage altruism, while constraints such as the "bystander effect" discourage it. Pro-social behavior can be increased by reducing ambiguity, increasing personal responsibility, and modeling desired behavior. Since collaboration is essential in producing successful vocal performances, the development of "people skills" and emotional intelligence is especially important to singers.

Abnormal Behavior

Occasionally, singers exhibit abnormal or disordered behaviors that deviate significantly from the norm. Major behavioral disorders include:

anxiety disorders — panic attacks, post-traumatic stress, phobias, and obsessive-compulsive disorder;

somatoform disorders — physical ailments without clear organic causes;

psychosexual disorders — disrupted or problematic sexual behavior;

dissociative disorders — amnesia, multiple personality, and depersonalization;

affective disorders — emotional experience, such as severe depression and mania, or bipolar disorder;

schizophrenic disorders — hallucination, delusions, and paranoia; and

personality disorders — antisocial, paranoid, schizoid, narcissistic, and borderline personality disorders.

Identifying and treating these disorders is the responsibility of medical experts rather than those who collaborate with singers.

The Singer's Personality

We reveal who we are by our speech: vocally, as projected in timbre, tempo, volume, range, dynamics; biologically, in terms of gender, age, and health; sociologically, in terms of ethnic or class background; and psycho-emotionally, according to mental and emotional intelligence. Since vocal dynamics project so much of one's true self, there's validity in the image of the voice as the "loudspeaker of the soul".

A singer's instrument becomes a reflection of personality because the voice and the personality are so intimately connected and intertwined (unlike the horn, for example, which can be taken up and put away). Singers express a wide range of emotions, boldly conveying the meaning of song texts directly to their audiences. In contrast, instrumentalists are typically not expected to perform as dramatically as singers, especially in terms of body movement, gestures, and facial expression.

Beyond talent and training, a vocal performer requires a strong sense of self, an intense personal drive to succeed, a positive, outgoing attitude, and an ability to relate well to people at all social levels. These factors contribute to the development of the "singer's personality".

One of the most attractive singing personalities today is mezzo-soprano Jennifer Larmore, who lives fully in the moment of each performance, and yet is also very thoughtful about what it takes to have a successful career as a singer. A desire to be rich or famous are the wrong reasons to go into a singing career, Ms. Larmore says, because audiences pick up on these emotions in the singer. In contrast, the pure love of singing and an intense desire to communicate project the singer in an attractive, winsome light.

Singers who concentrate on ensemble performance (opera, oratorio, chamber ensembles) require even more cooperative and collaborative skill than the singers working in less demanding situations. The well-balanced singer in all cases needs to have a thorough understanding of self, can perceive reality accurately, and can give passionate attention to the pursuit of worthwhile goals.

Notable Quotes: The Singer as Psychologist

How do you manage your emotions?

> If you go into a singing career to be famous, or to be rich, those are the wrong reasons. . . That in itself, I think, brings along some type of negativism, and people feel it . . . When you sing, what comes out in your voice? Your soul! It's a way of exposing your emotions, and the person you are. . . At the end of the day (of performing) I can go to bed and feel good about my life, and about what I'm doing, and about my future. I'll have so many good memories when I'm old and gray, at the nursing home. — Jennifer Larmore

Do you ever experience anxiety or stage fright?

> I am always living with fear. At the end of this afternoon, I will conduct *Samson et Dalila* [by Saint-Saëns]. But before that, I really have to find two hours to work on *The Queen of Spades* [by Tchaikovsky]. Russian, which is already formidable to pronounce, is proving even worse to memorize. Right now, I wake up in the middle of the night because I feel some sentences are escaping me. I switch on the light. I take the score and I work. Otherwise, my anxiety would be such that I would not be able to sleep. It does not matter; my whole life has been this way. In this trade, it is impossible to concentrate exclusively on the work you are singing or conducting [at the moment]. You have to live the following [role] at the same time.
> — Plácido Domingo

Chapter 3

The Singer as Reconciler of Opposites

How Singers Achieve Balanced Voice Quality

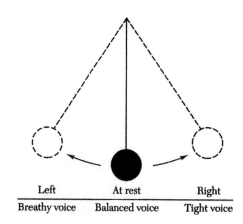

A pendulum in the "at rest" position (center) represents balanced singing. Swings of the pendulum to the right and left of center represent degrees of variation from a singer's ideal voice quality, or "balanced voice". For example, a tight-voiced singer (pendulum right) may be advised to counteract excessive vocal tension by working toward the opposite extreme of relaxation or breathiness (represented by pendulum left). The "at rest" pendulum represents the reconciliation of opposites (including brilliance and warmth, lightness and heaviness, intensity and relaxation, words and tone, vowels and consonants, releasing and focusing).

Why Study Opposites?

I became acquainted with the theory of opposites years ago after a careful study of William Vennard's *Singing: The Mechanism and The Technique* (1967) in preparation for teaching a vocal pedagogy class at the University of Minnesota. Since that initial "awakening", I've continued my quest to understand how the reconciliation of opposites can be applied in developing efficient vocal production and learning and performing challenging classical vocal repertoire.

While performing with the Minnesota Opera in the 1970s, I had the good fortune to work with Wesley Balk, an innovative stage director who authored four significant books aimed at singers and actors. In *The Complete Singing Actor* (1977) and *Performing Power* (1985), Balk developed his theory and showed how to integrate opposites in performance. After this formative learning period, I became increasingly aware of opposites in nature, and, more importantly, of how one must reconcile them to live a balanced life and achieve a balanced approach to singing.

Philosophical Basis for Opposites

The concept of opposites is rooted in philosophical dualism, which is any theory based on two contrasting aspects. Dualism is prevalent in the history of Western philosophy, beginning with ancient Greek philosophers, including Pythagoras, who found evidence for opposites in astronomy, geometry, music, architecture, acoustics, psychology, biology, and mechanics. Pythagoras' Table of Opposites (seen on the next page) includes ten pairs of contraries (the number 10 was considered a perfect number). One of anything is a unity; but two or more of anything creates tension and opposition. The clapping of two hands illustrates the principle of reconciliation of opposites, because even though two hands clap together only one sound is produced.

PYTHAGORAS' TABLE OF OPPOSITES	
Limited	Unlimited
Odd	Even
Unity	Plurality
Right	Left
Male	Female
At Rest	In Motion
Straight	Curved
Light	Dark
Good	Evil
Square	Oblong

Pythagoras' Table of Opposites was described by Aristotle, who offered a "golden mean" for reconciling Pythagorean Opposites as well as Plato's dualism of "reality" (souls) and "appearances" (bodies). Dualism in Western philosophy is also evident in St. Augustine's "City of God" contrasted with his "City of Man", in Descartes' concept of mind versus matter, in Hegel's synthesis of opposites resulting from the clash of thesis and antithesis, in Dewey's dualism between spirit and nature, and in Sartre's existentialism contrasting "beingness" with "nothingness".

While Western culture in the Middle Ages elevated the world of souls ("being"), Renaissance humanists celebrated the world of action ("becoming"). The modern world's interest in the secular world of action (*vita activa*) heralded a cultural retreat from the world of contemplation (*vita contemplativa*), and with it a celebration of wealth and worldly accomplishments (inventions, conquests, learning, and the like). But modern civilization may, in turn, have taken the secular path to an extreme, as our modern preoccupation with accomplishment (product) has tended to disparage or even extinguish the role of the soul or the spiritual dimension.

Today we continue to express our need for "balance", as evidenced by our attraction to Eastern philosophies that teach a state of "non-doing" or "being". This has been a compensatory movement, as the customary Western objective of achieving a "product" (ends, performance) is often valued more than the enjoyment and mastery of "process" (means, practice) — which, in a balanced view, can be sufficient unto itself.

In Eastern philosophy, dualism is epitomized by the yin-yang principle expressing contrasts and differences, as in classical Taoism. While "yin" (passive, negative) and "yang" (active, positive) are in direct relationship to each other, they are opposites. In China the yin-yang concept is often referred to as describing interactions among concrete things, but is also thought of as an image of the ideal relation between body and soul of the individual human being.

According to Taoist philosophy, personality integration is achieved through living a simple life, a view that holds special significance in an increasingly complex world. A mind stuffed full of knowledge, cleverness, and abstract ideas tends to chase things that don't matter or even exist. For example, in a Taoist landscape painting, emptiness is the space that's not filled. Debussy unknowingly held a Taoist viewpoint when he claimed, "Music is the space between the notes".

The modern trend of using meditation strategies is based on the belief that emptiness cleans out a cluttered mind and renews spiritual energy. In the *Tao Te Ching* (48th Chapter) one reads: "To attain knowledge, add things every day;

to attain wisdom, remove things every day." This saying implies that one must both add positive information and remove negative information.

Scientific Basis for Opposites

The concept of opposites derives from the two-part structure of the human brain. Though the brain's two lobes perform specialized tasks or functions, they collaborate in negotiating complex tasks. The *left hemisphere* sorts and orders individual pieces of information, and excels in such functions as reading, speaking, pitch and rhythm discrimination, analytical thought, conscious mental processes, and control over the body's right side. In contrast, the *right hemisphere* perceives stimuli contextually and holistically, and dominates in such functions as intuition, visual-spatial relationships, timbre processing, imagination, creativity, expressiveness, and control over the body's left side. A singer must be able to utilize both hemispheres in balanced efficiency.

PET (positron emission tomography) scans and MRI (magnetic resonance imaging) scans have shown that pitch and rhythm processing occurs primarily in the left hemisphere and timbre processing primarily in the right hemisphere of the brain. The frontal brain and cerebellum activate when subjects are unfamiliar with the stimulus or need to coordinate short-term memory and long- term memory retrieval/encoding. (Potter, 2000)

The two-part brain is essentially a coping mechanism. Its agility and complexity are demonstrated when it copes with ambiguity, as it must in vocal performance. Personal integration (reconciliation of opposites) can occur in various aspects of life, such as one's internal-external self, being-doing states, introvert-extrovert characteristics, analytical-intuitive learning techniques, liberal-conservative political views, past-future horizons, spiritual-materialistic desires, and ugly-beautiful aesthetic choices.

Practical Applications in Singing

The reconciliation of opposites in singing involves coordination of the entire vocal process. Specifically, the singer's task is to coordinate volition (intent), a psycho-emotional act, with the physiological areas of *respiration* (breath management), *phonation* (vocal-fold vibration), *resonation* (tonal enhancement), and *articulation* (diction). Since the coordination of these areas is greatly dependent upon one's physical state, the importance of physical relaxation, good health, and body alignment cannot be exaggerated. The ultimate goal is to seek, discover, and develop a balanced approach in all areas of singing, as well as in life.

Learning to reconcile relaxation with tension is particularly difficult because muscles work in opposites; one set activating (*agonists*) while the opposing set (*antagonists*) relaxes. This process, *muscular antagonism*, is the basis for all muscle activity. Thus, while the singer's body must remain upwardly stretched (sternum high, rib cage expanded), vitalized and buoyant, the articulating organs (jaw, tongue, lips, etc.) must remain relaxed, while at the same time nimbly and flexibly active.

In *respiration* singers must reconcile the phases of inhalation and exhalation. During a complete breathing cycle (inhalation, suspension, exhalation, and recovery) various torso muscles alternate between being active and passive. For example, muscles tend to be more relaxed during the inhalation phase and more engaged during the exhalation (vocalization) phase, largely depending on the requisite breath requirements (volume, range, length) for each musical phrase. These opposing forces are partially balanced by the "gesture of inhalation" — a sensation somewhat like a sustained suspension breath phase — that helps retard the expulsion of breath in producing vocalized tone.

Phonation, which involves vocal-fold oscillation in response to breath-flow, can be represented at the extremes by pressed and breathy phonation. There are two contrasting undesirable approaches in initiating tone, or *onset* of tone. *Pressed onset* occurs when the vocal folds are tightly brought together (adducted), effectively damming the breath, with the tone exploding abruptly. Some rock singers use this type of onset frequently in stressful singing. In contrast, *breathy onset* occurs when breath is released through loosely adducted vocal folds, resulting in an airy ("h-h-h") sound, a production often heard in young singers. The ideal, of course, is a *coordinated onset*, as occurs in hearty laughter and efficient vocal technique, as demonstrated by prominent Italian-like opera singers.

In addition, there are three major types of phonation. In *pressed phonation* the vocal folds are drawn together too tightly, thereby creating a hard-sounding, tight tone. In *breathy phonation* the vocal folds are loosely drawn together, thus producing a sustained airy-sounding tone. The ideal, balanced phonation is known as *flow phonation*, characterized by a vocal-fold closure that is neither too tight nor too loose. The result is a flowing tone that seems to ride on the breath.

Resonation, which is largely dependent on the alignment and shape of the vocal tract (throat, mouth, and nasal cavities), in conjunction with vocal-fold oscillation, is associated with the production of tone quality or *timbre*, a product of complex acoustical energies. When resonation and phonation conditions are maximized, the *harmonic spectrum* (overtone series) is well balanced between highs (tweeters) and lows (woofers), and the coordinated result is *chiaroscuro*, the bright-dark (balanced opposites) tone prized by Italian vocal pedagogues. In contrast, both excessively bright and dark tones are indications of inefficient singing.

The topic of voice *registration* is also relevant to this discussion. As most vocal authorities concur, there are two contrasting registers: *head (loft, light mechanism) voice* and *chest (modal, heavy mechanism) voice*. In addition, many authorities ascribe to a *middle (mixed) register*, which is considered a blend of head and chest registers. When a voice is uncoordinated, the two major registers are very apparent, with the chest or low-voice mechanism sounding heavy and thick, and the head or high-voice mechanism sounding light and thin. However, when a singer's registers are coordinated, there is a seamless blend from top to bottom, with no bumps, cracks, or gross changes in tonal quality. In effect, the best qualities of head and chest registers are integrated, providing strength and fullness in conjunction with lightness and sweetness of tone.

Articulation refers to the production of vowels and consonants to form words and communicate meaning. In voice study, vowels and consonants are frequently thought of as complementary opposites. *Vowels* provide varying shades of sustained tonal qualities (colors, timbres), while *consonants* (formed by airflow being interrupted through closure, diversion, and constriction of the articulating organs) provide clarification and projection of texts.

Related to this vowel-consonant encounter is the ongoing dualistic struggle regarding the importance of beautiful singing tone versus textual concerns. The two opposing camps are opera singers (as epitomized by Joan Sutherland and Luciano Pavarotti) and lieder singers (represented by Gerard Souzay and Elly Ameling). Two examples of contemporary singers who manage both opera and art song, voice and text, are Renée Fleming and Bryn Terfel.

There are other areas of opposites in singing that must be reconciled. For instance, soft (*piano*) singing must be balanced with loud (*forte*) singing, resulting in a predominant norm of *mezzo piano* and *mezzo forte* dynamic levels. Moreover, vibrato patterns need to be stabilized at 6-7 pulses per second, rather than functioning aberrantly at the extremes, either in excess of 8 (bleat) or less than 5 (wobble). Other desirable skills include the ability to sing fast (*coloratura*) or slow (*sostenuto*), powerfully or tenderly, high or low, and with true intonation, neither flat nor sharp in pitch.

The "reconciliation of opposites" concept in singing is epitomized by the *appoggio* technique of traditional Italian vocal pedagogy. Meaning, literally, "to lean", *appoggio* refers to the "hooked-up" vocal effect that is achieved through the interdependence and synergy of the entire vocal mechanism. As the noted Italian vocal pedagogue G. B. Lamperti stated: "The singing voice in reality is born of the clash of opposing principles, the tension of conflicting forces, brought to an equilibrium "(Brown 1973, p. 3). As Jeremy Bentham (1748-1832) put it, "The mark of a first-rate mind is that it can maintain two contradictory ideas at one time."

Notable Quotes: The Singer as Reconciler of Opposites

How did you develop such a well-balanced voice, with such consistency and control in range, resonance, registration, and dynamics?

> I had to learn to do the high, floating pianissimos. The key was to realize that we have to work against our natural tendencies, which in singing softly is to grab or hold with the throat to try and stop the flow of sound and the flow of breath when, in fact, you have to allow the flow to continue. A very good exercise

that I practice is the *messa di voce* on all pitches going up chromatically and back down again. There is a slightly different use of resonance, a more focused use of resonance. It's important to learn how to balance the change in resonance. When you decrescendo, think of the resonances going up and release from the bottom up. There is also a change in the flow of breath. It requires a lot of experimentation, and for sopranos, listening to Montserrat Caballé. The problem of holding is one of the hardest things to fix. For a good legato, work on anything with a glissando to get a sense of the continuation of the line. It takes practice and experience. — Renée Fleming

Are American composers aware of opposites when composing?

An American composer is always more interesting in the context of his or her own period, or when paired with a completely contrasting voice. But that's part of the American spirit — to show where the round side of the edge is, and vice versa. As a culture, we're always sort of mesmerized by opposites. — Thomas Hampson

Chapter 4

The Singer as Vocal Athlete

Meeting the Demands of Athletic Singing

Within the vocal community singing is recognized as an extremely demanding profession — mentally, emotionally, and physically. Hectic contemporary lifestyles stress singers frequently to the point of exhaustion. This chapter addresses ways singers can achieve the status of "vocal athlete" in their quest to develop and maintain mind-body wellness. The rationale is simple: physical health profoundly influences our emotional state, energy level, appearance, social behavior, stress-coping ability, and vocal condition.

The complex mind-body coordination required of solo vocal performers might be compared to the intricate performances of Olympic-level athletes, notably figure skaters. Since a singer's total vocal instrument is his or her body, rigorous mental and physical conditioning are needed to develop sufficient energy for coping with challenging performances that include leading opera roles and full-length recitals. Energy, which may be thought of as the biological force that enables zestful living, is a requisite for helping motivated singers achieve their professional goals.

Because the vocal athlete must generate high energy levels for singing, personal testimonies are offered throughout this chapter regarding the strategies my wife, Bettye, and I have used to remain physically fit and in good health into our mid 60s. We both wish we'd known during our youth what we now know about nutrition and exercise; we'd be even better off if we'd started earlier with the healthy habits we now practice regularly.

In this chapter we consider ways to increase energy reserves, beginning with nutrition, then physical fitness, and finally psycho-emotional wellness. We will demonstrate how a vocal athlete's disciplined, constructive behavior in developing and maintaining a healthy lifestyle results in habits that encourage good vocal hygiene.

Fueling Energy: Diet and Nutrition

Many singers suffer — as does the general U.S. population — from either obesity or extreme thinness caused by eating disorders. Though a singer's physical appearance is always an important issue, especially in opera, the overriding concern is maintaining good health through proper nutrition, which is the result of practicing appropriate eating and drinking habits. When one's weight fails to fall within prescribed medical guidelines, the cause is often unhealthy eating and drinking habits combined with insufficient physical activity and/or psycho-emotional problems.

Everyone is familiar with the generally accepted advice regarding sensible eating habits. DO adhere to diet programs (such as Dean Ornish's "Life Choice" program and Walter C. Willett's "Healthy Eating Pyramid") that recommend a well-balanced and varied diet based on the major food groups: vegetables, fruits, lean meats, dairy products, etc. Also, doctor-recommended vitamin and mineral supplements may be needed — at minimum a single all-purpose multi-vitamin. DON'T adhere to fad diets that emphasize particular food groups to the exclusion of others, consume large quantities of alcoholic or caffeine loaded beverages, or "pig out" on junk foods, which are loaded with fats and sugars.

One must simply use common sense in matters of food and drink intake, chiefly by consuming healthy, well-balanced meals in limited proportions at regular intervals and by carefully avoiding late-night meals prior to sleeping (to avoid *gastric reflux*). But even though everyone knows what to do, getting started and persevering with a healthy diet takes considerable motivation and self-discipline.

Assuming one has the requisite knowledge, resources, and motivation to consume healthy food and drink, the most effective way to control what one eats is to dine at home as frequently as possible. Singers who travel must often eat in restaurants or cafeterias, which often presents problems in finding healthy options (especially in fast-food restaurants). Learning about the contents of particular dishes served in restaurants usually requires some detective work, and most people simply don't want to make the effort. However, when eating at home and preparing your own meals, there's little excuse for not eating healthily.

My wife and I are very careful to select foods and beverages that are nutritious and easy to prepare, as neither of us is enthusiastic about preparing gourmet meals. We generally seek fresh, frozen, or canned vegetables and fruits aimed at health-conscious consumers. For instance, some types of canned salmon provide easy-to-prepare, healthy seafood meals. And whole-grain breads and cereals (oatmeal, bran), nuts, and fruits (bananas, prunes, apricots, etc.)

create get-up-and-go breakfasts. Soups and whole-grain pastas, whole-grain brown rice served with steamed or stir-fried mixed vegetables, nuts, and small bits of chicken serve as tasty, filling meals. For beverages we stick mostly to citrus juices, decaffeinated teas (green, black, herbal), skim milk, and water.

As to whether people should take supplementary minerals and vitamins, there is consistent research to suggest that most people benefit from taking a daily multi-vitamin, especially since the typical American diet fails to provide all the daily essential vitamins and minerals in the quantities needed for healthy living. Based on the latest findings, my wife and I err on the side of cautionary supplementation.

The final word on diet and nutrition is the old (but highly motivating) cliché, "You are what you eat", a truism well worth bearing in mind.

Developing Energy: Fitness and Exercise

Together with good nutrition, staying physically active is perhaps the single most important factor in maintaining a well-conditioned body. One should establish a habit of exercising regularly (from twenty to forty-plus minutes per day), alternating between *aerobic* activities, such as vigorous walking, swimming, and bicycling to build cardiovascular stamina, and *anaerobic* activities, such as muscle stretching, calisthenics, and weight-lifting (which increase muscle flexibility and power).

Of course, before undertaking any new exercise program, one should be sure to have a thorough physical examination by a doctor. Also, proceed carefully when searching for an exercise program that suits your particular situation and needs. The goal should be to achieve a well-balanced, safe exercise regimen that you can take with you everywhere.

My personal experience with physical conditioning began with some brief, lightweight exercise in my mid 20s: push-ups, sit-ups, and related muscle-toning exercises. But a serious interest in overall physical conditioning didn't occur until I reached my early 40s. At that time, while on vacation in Europe, my 13-year-old son and I climbed a small mountain in Scotland. While scrambling to keep up with him on some steep slopes, I thought I might have a heart attack. Never before had I been so physically stressed. That experience turned out to be a wake-up call, a warning to improve my physical conditioning. However, for reasons I can't recall, I procrastinated for another two years.

Then one day I decided to run around the block, and was chagrined to discover I couldn't do it without gasping for air. Not long after that humiliating experience, I was stuck at my university office without a ride home. It was a lovely day, so I decided to walk the 5 miles. As I was in my typical hurry-along mode, I decided to alternate slow running with fast walking. Amazingly, I made it home safely, without being too fatigued. I gradually became addicted to running, sometimes up to 6 miles a day, and ever since I've been a faithful exercise nut. Perhaps because of ill pacing and lack of proper warm-ups, I developed "Achilles Heel" and painful hip-joint conditions from running, so I have reduced the distance to 3-4 miles per walk-run, a pattern that has worked well for several years.

For the past decade my daily exercise routine has varied, but now typically begins around 5:30-6:00 a.m., and includes four mornings per week of 45-minute aerobic workouts on our home treadmill (at a 10 percent grade for 3 miles), and two mornings per week of 35-minute anaerobic workouts that includes stretching, back exercises, and moderate weight-lifting, followed by 22 minutes on the treadmill (on a 10 percent grade for 1.5 miles). In addition, I end each session with a two-minute Tai Chi routine I learned from observing a master practitioner. In general, I try to stay as active as possible by pursuing such recreational sports as hiking and biking, and tending to normal household chores such as shoveling snow, cutting grass, and raking leaves. I've gladly adopted as my exercise credo the popular cliché, "Use it or lose it!"

Finally, one shouldn't overlook the opportunity to walk whenever possible. All too often, when using the stairways in the University parking ramp or School of Music complex, I pass students (even young teachers) who are waiting for elevators to transport them a couple of floors, subsequently missing a wonderful opportunity for a mild stairway workout. Rather than looking for ways to save on walking, I prefer to find reasons to walk, including walking around the three floors of the music building complex and adjoining campus whenever I have a free moment.

Restoring Energy: Rest, Relaxation, and Recreation

While some ambitious singers thrive on multi-tasked schedules and are able to cope with prolonged stress, most vocal performers need regular breaks from professional activities, especially when energy levels are low. What can be done to assure our "batteries" are fully charged?

Since good health provides the wherewithal to pursue personal goals with vigor and vitality, our first priority is to do everything possible to maintain it, beginning with adequate nutrition and regular exercise. Next, it's a matter of getting sufficient rest, beginning with a good night's sleep lasting 7-8 hours, in addition to short daily periods of relaxation, particularly 1-3 hours prior to bedtime.

My general practice is to cease all professional activity at 6 p.m., eat supper, and then enjoy relaxing activities such as reading, watching TV or a movie. Though this routine may be anathema to young singers, not to mention almost impossible to achieve due to a busy performing and social lifestyle, it is crucial to unwind prior to bedtime. If, like me, you are an "early-to-bed, early-to-rise" type, the singer's lifestyle can present problems. As a youth I was accustomed to staying up late and awakening later, and it is a common pattern of the young to burn the candle on both ends, as the saying goes.

For singers with hectic schedules, making time for restorative functions takes commitment and planning. Nevertheless, daily and weekly vacations from work routines to pursue pleasurable activities will help reduce stress and restore energy levels. It's important to maintain a lifestyle that keeps work and play in balance, permitting healthy mind-body function.

Preserving Your Voice: Habits of Good Hygiene

Like all humans, singers develop a variety of ailments, some short-term (colds) and others long-term (serious illnesses), any of which can adversely affect the vocal instrument. Inexplicably, some "iron-voiced" singers manage to sing through most afflictions, while their more sensitive colleagues are rendered voiceless under similar conditions. Low-voice types seem to handle vocal difficulties better than their high-voice counterparts, possibly because of challenging repertoire that requires extensive vocal ranges and high-lying *tessitura* (note range), but also because of psychophysical factors, such as personality type and body size. Each singer needs to become aware of his or her mind-body strengths and limitations, and do everything possible to work within them.

Because of the wide prevalence of mind-body altering substances in contemporary society, I would be remiss if

I failed to comment on their effects on individuals, their loved ones, and society as a whole. First, I believe that any substance that alters natural mind-body functioning is inherently bad for human consumption. For instance, regardless of the recently touted benefits of ingesting moderate amounts of wine, or the so-called relaxing benefits of alcoholic beverages, marijuana, and other drugs, including steroids, I still think we have less to gain than to lose in using such substances. Not for one minute do I regret having abstained from experimenting with any of them, with the exception of puffing on a few cigarettes as a kid (cough, cough), and sipping occasional alcoholic drinks (mostly wine) on social occasions.

For the most part, as far as tobacco, alcohol, and drugs are concerned, I consider myself a near teetotaler. Does this mean that I've missed out on the joys of living? Absolutely not! Please take my word for it that it's possible to have a full, meaningful life without resorting to (or depending upon) potentially harmful substances!

Summary and Conclusion

To summarize, we've been reminded that good food and drink keep our biological systems operational; that exercise and overall fitness strengthen our mind-body systems for strenuous activity; and that our energy is replenished through rest, relaxation, and recreation. Finally, we reviewed some ways to conserve and protect our vocal instrument through good vocal hygiene.

Singers who adopt and adhere to these guidelines will surely enhance their prospects for developing and maintaining long-term vocal careers. And, in receiving the highest form of professional recognition, they will earn the right to be known as "vocal athletes."

DO'S AND DON'TS OF VOCAL HEALTH

DO . . .

- Consume a variety of nutritious foods and beverages
- Attain and maintain physical fitness with regular aerobic and muscle-toning workouts
- Obtain sufficient rest, sleep, and recreation
- Maintain a humid environment (40-50 percent humidity)
- Maintain body hydration by drinking 7-9 glasses of liquids daily
- Use efficient vocal technique in speech and singing
- Use the voice judiciously
- Wash hands frequently, and avoid rubbing eyes and probing nose

DON'T . . .

- Inhale or ingest harmful substances, such as caffeine, alcohol, recreational drugs, tobacco, and polluted air
- Pursue an overly stressful lifestyle
- Make physical contact with persons with contagious diseases
- Work or live in noisy, polluted environments
- Speak too much or too loudly, especially in noisy environments
- Scream or clear the throat excessively
- Use over-the-counter preparations for colds and allergies, especially antihistamines

Notable Quotes: The Singer as Athlete

How do you maintain healthy vocalism in the midst of a demanding performance schedule?

> This is such a high-risk business. We're darting all over the place from engagement to engagement and I'm convinced they pay you for what that costs you in your body and your mind. One day you're in South America and the next you're in Alaska and you're trying to keep your instrument healthy under all of those crazy conditions. That's what the challenge is, that's what technique is all about, that's what all those years in the conservatory are preparing you for — this lifestyle that is ahead of you. — Denyce Graves

Do you do anything to get your body ready for vocal performance?

> Yoga. I've always insisted that you have to stretch and activate the musculature of your body before you attempt to make it work by singing. I find my warm-ups are shorter if the body is awake and alive and flexible. I've been in situations where I've been told, "So-and-so is sick. You've got to be in your dressing room in five minutes." What do you do in five minutes to get ready? I stretch and I breathe, and then I can be on top of my voice. – Cynthia Lawrence

What effect does a singer's weight and size have on his or her career?

> In the August 2002 issue of *Opera News*, John Simon [theater critic of *New York* magazine] said largeness in a man bespeaks masculinity, whereas fatness in a woman bespeaks the opposite of femininity. I didn't

even know who this John Simon was until I read that. I think he has a narrow view — he is small-minded, he sees beauty only one way and he's very limited. There's no point in getting upset about something like that, even though this attitude towards heavy people is the last bastion of open discrimination in our society. Get this: the management of Covent Garden just released me from my contract for *Ariadne auf Naxos* in 2004. They simply said I was too fat! It makes me so angry. Since then I've lost 45 pounds. Let's say I'm determined to lose more with [the assistance of] my personal trainer, with a combination of nutrition and workouts. I'm actually lifting weights!
— Deborah Voigt

Do you make time for rest and recreational activities in the midst of your hectic performing career?

I work during six or seven months and the rest is for my private life. Taking time off is absolutely necessary in order to keep one's balance. My time off is spread out over the year, perhaps a month, or a week between engagements. It depends on the project. Taking it all at once would mean starting from scratch each time. — Cecilia Bartoli

What do the critics say about Samuel Ramey's athleticism?

Boris Godunov (title role) with The Washington Opera: ". . . his electrical presence, his bounding athleticism. . . . (Tim Page, *Washington Post*)

Faust (role of Méphistophélès) with the Lyric Opera of Chicago: ". . . prancing about the stage with virile, athletic glee. . . He commands the stage even when standing still." (John von Rhein, *Chicago Tribune*)

Faust (role of Méphistophélès) with the Metropolitan Opera: ". . . Samuel Ramey performs with agility; this rare athletic bass can swing with natural ease through Gounod's most awkward lines, just as he swings around the stage." (Paul Griffiths, *The New York Times*)

The Rake's Progress (role of Nick Shadow) with the Lyric Opera of Chicago: "Lean and angular in his tight black knee britches and tails, he sings with an assured, authoritative manner that demands Rakewell's obedience." (Wynne Delacoma, *Chicago Sun-Times*)

Chapter 5

The Singer as Aural Processor

Though singers conscientiously give considerable attention to voice improvement and care, their sense of hearing is often taken for granted. Good hearing is essential for matching pitches, monitoring vocal quality, and providing feedback in making appropriate adjustments during singing. Typically, the crucial role of the ear in singing becomes apparent only when singers experience illnesses or adverse conditions that affect hearing. This general oversight becomes very evident when perusing the many books on singing, most of which reveal little information about the ear's essential role in singing. But increasing numbers of singers, voice scientists, and teachers of singing are beginning to explore the ear's vital role in singing, as well as its influence in the broader areas of learning and behavior.

The Effects of Noise Pollution on Hearing and Singing

One explanation for the growing awareness of hearing can be traced to the ever-increasing amounts of noise pollution observed over the last 150 years, beginning with the industrial revolution and continuing through the technological evolution. Prior to the development of large machinery, the human environment was relatively noise-free. But, beginning in the early nineteenth century, concentrated urban societies gradually came under attack by a deafening din of city noises, particularly in developing countries, with the U.S. and Europe at the forefront.

It is a sad reality that listening to and performing loud music can have a deleterious effect on hearing. Long-term exposure to loud music has been shown to cause hearing loss among rock singers, orchestral musicians, and listeners. Of particular concern are youths who install earth-shaking sound systems in their cars, then cruise around blasting the delicate nerves and senses of everyone within earshot.

Looking back, I see that my teen years predated high-powered sound systems. Aside from school dances, my exposure to loud music has been limited to performances with orchestras and choirs (when decibel levels rarely reached dangerous levels), and occasional studies of large musical works when I used earphones in listening to recordings. My most unpleasant noise exposure has probably been limited to lawn mower engines, power tools, and the like. I'm lucky to have retained most of my hearing, with the typical loss of some high frequency pitches at my ripe age. Though I have *tinnitus* (ear ringing), it isn't to the point of being a real bother. On the other hand, I know many persons — young and old — who have significant hearing loss, primarily attributed to long bouts of ongoing noise pollution. My strategy is to do everything possible to avoid situations where loud noise is expected, including large public events where everyone is yelling. Whenever possible, I wear earplugs to protect my hearing when exposed to prolonged loud noise, even at movie theaters, where the sound is often deafening.

Urban environments today are deafening, but the noise-making will continue to increase until public awareness leads to pressure for laws and regulations against noise pollution. Until then, ever-larger numbers of youth will experience significant hearing loss by the time they reach their adult years.

The effects of noise on hearing are determined by such factors as level, frequency, composition, duration, distribution of exposure, and length of long-term exposure. In terms of loudness, or decibels, the general rule is that a sound pressure level of 120 dB is uncomfortably loud for most people, and that exposure to levels in excess of 85-90 dB for sustained periods can result in permanent hearing loss. Hearing loss in the 3000-6000 Hertz (Hz) range frequently goes unnoticed, because these frequencies occur mostly above the normal speaking and singing range. But when hearing loss affects the 2000-4000 Hz range, some speech and singing sounds may not be discernable. Diminished capacity in this latter range is usually associated with the aging process, although hearing loss is probably aggravated by recurring, pervasive noise pollution. In the worst cases, the lower frequency ranges associated with speech and singing are affected, and communication skills are greatly diminished.

The Hearing Mechanism and How it Works

Understanding hearing loss begins with a working knowledge of the marvelous hearing organ — "the road to the heart" as Voltaire described it. There are four factors that determine the creation and perception of sound: (1) a force to set a vibrator in action; (2) a vibrator; (3) a medium to convey the wave motion originating from the vibrator; and (4) a receptor mechanism that can receive and interpret the propagated wave's energy. The human auditory system is comprised of three principal parts: the outer ear, the middle ear, and the inner ear.

The *outer ear* is divided into two parts: the auricle (or *pinna*), a trumpet-bell receptor located on the side of the head, and the tube or external auditory canal that leads from the opening *(meatus)* of the auricle to the temporal bone. The middle ear begins with the eardrum *(tympanic membrane)*, which stretches across the end of the external ear canal, separating it from the middle ear.

The *middle ear*, a small cavity in the temporal bone, consists of three auditory *ossicles*, a *malleus* (hammer), an *incus* (anvil), and a *stapes* (stirrup), all of which form a bony bridge from the external to the inner ear that is connected by ligaments and muscles. The chamber of the middle ear is filled with air and is connected to the throat by the Eustachian tube, which helps equalize air pressure on both sides of the eardrum.

Anatomy of the Ear

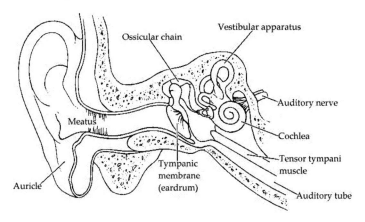

The *inner ear* — a bony, membranous labyrinth — is filled with fluid. The inner ear is divided into two parts: the *vestibular apparatus*, which serves as a principal balancing mechanism for the body; and the *cochlea*, which contains over 15,000 minute, hair-like cells called *the organ of Corti*. Finally, the acoustic nerve (the eighth cranial nerve) leads from the inner ear to the brain, functioning as the conduit for neural impulses which the brain interprets as sound.

The way we hear can be broken down into a simplified explanation. First, sound waves enter the outer ear and travel through the external ear canal. Upon reaching the eardrum (tympanic membrane) the sound waves (vibrations) are then transferred via the middle ear's auditory ossicles over the bony bridge formed by the malleus, incus, and stapes. When the vibrations reach the membranes over the openings of the inner ear (cochlea), they cause the fluid of the inner ear to be set in motion. These hydrodynamic waves create a shearing motion (similar to wind blowing over a wheat field), in turn exciting the inner and outer hair nerve cells located in the *organ of Corti*, which functions as the switchboard of the auditory system. Finally, when electrochemical impulses transmitted via the acoustic nerve reach the brain, the impacting impulses result in the sensation of hearing.

Hearing, Listening, and Singing

There are two principal ways singers hear their own voices; first, through the external ears (auricles); and, second, through bone conduction, from skull bone to the inner ear's bony mass. In addition, singers are generally tuned into kinesthetic sensations caused by sound vibrations experienced primarily in the facial bones, but also including other areas in the head, neck, and upper torso. In fact, some research supports the idea that speech and singing rely heavily on the hearing mechanism — in conjunction with the entire body — for effective auditory feedback, interpretation, and communication.

In the 1950s Dr. Alfred Tomatis, a renowned French ear, nose, and throat (ENT) specialist, made the profound discovery that the ear-brain connection controls voice production and language, and that the ear (listening process) actually determines the harmonics produced in a tone. He also claimed that voice quality is primarily controlled by the right (leading) ear, because it is generally more adapted to controlling the singing voice, instrument playing, speech production, and tuning. Throughout his ongoing clinical observations and experiments Tomatis discovered that hearing also plays a significant role in other major areas of human development, including communication skills, facility with spoken and written language, attention span, written language, and basic learning skills. Further support for Tomatis's claims was initially provided by the rigorous research of the highly regarded French scientist, Raoul Husson.

Paul Madaule, an ardent advocate of the *Tomatis Method* and director of The Listening Centre in Toronto, Canada, makes a sharp distinction between *hearing*, which may be defined as the passive reception of sound, and *listening*, which he considers an active process involving selection of essential and desirable sounds while screening out unessential and unwanted sounds. Moreover, listening involves both the perception of external sounds and the sound of one's own voice. Language acquisition begins with children hearing environmental sounds, then mimicking and modeling selective sounds as needed.

Madaule claims that the same process occurs in singing, which he believes to be the best type of listening training because it develops auditory control through reinforcement and fine-tuning. The process of vocal production begins with volition, or intention to utter a sound. Next, instant, intricate, and complex mind-body interactions create neural impulses that activate appropriate bodily responses, beginning with air being expelled from the lungs through the trachea to the larynx, where the vocal folds vibrate in response to airflow. Finally, the fundamental buzz tone of the vocal folds is enhanced with resonance, which is generated in the vocal tract and shaped by the speech articulators into vowels and consonants, words, and, ultimately, expressive communication.

Self-listening and audio-vocal control begin at the same point as vocal-fold sound production. Tomatis stressed that audio-vocal control consists of two parts. The first involves the transmission of vocal-fold vibration to the body's bone structure and to the inner ear by bone conduction. This ear-voice feedback alerts the brain that a tone needs proper shaping by the vocal tract, and bone-conducted audio-voice control supplies the singer with the unique kinesthetic sensation of his or her voice. The second part of audio-vocal control involves sound traveling through the vocal tract and exiting the mouth, where the ear receives the sound through air conduction. The time lapse between bone and air conduction allows singers a split second to adjust numerous body parts — bones, muscles, and ligaments — by means of positioning, shaping, and tensing. Fine-tuned adjustments of speech articulators produce various vocal inflections that lead to enhanced expression. Of course, a deficiency in any area of the audio-vocal feedback loop will negatively affect vocal production and tone quality.

Tomatis also emphasized that the inner ear's two systems are contrasting yet mutually supportive systems that work together harmoniously. The *cochlear system* deals with sound perception, which includes melody and lyrics, while the *vestibular system* deals with physical balance, which involves such areas as posture, rhythm, and movement. Traditionally, singers have tended to concentrate more on developing and improving aural qualities, but more attention is now being focused on the equally important vestibular system, the so-called "ear of the body", which contributes to the sense of being "grounded" or "centered".

In training people to become better listeners, the Tomatis Method uses sound stimulation to exercise the ear. An audio device called the Electronic Ear was developed by Tomatis to create an ear-voice feedback loop. In addition to using recorded instrumental and vocal music, the device directs attention to the singer's voice, which is recorded by microphone, processed through the Electronic Ear, and then transmitted through head phones into the singer's ear for self-listening. Self-corrective exercises are then used to strengthen audio-vocal control, including work on posture and humming, which stimulates vibrations in the torso and head through bone conduction. The goal is to help the singer experience listening as a kinesthetic, tactile step in effective voice production.

The pervasive confusion concerning tone deafness — the inability to sing on pitch — is directly addressed by the Tomatis Method's emphasis on improving hearing. One notable hearing expert, W. Dixon Ward, a former Professor of Communication Disorders at the University of Minnesota, was quoted as saying: "One is not born tone deaf but becomes tone deaf — based on psychological processes associated with early learning . . . in a sense we are all born with perfect pitch and it is trained out of us". The Tomatis Method recognizes this unfortunate loss, and seeks to reestablish hearing skills as a way to improve vocalism.

Hearing Disorders: Prevention and Cure

The most prevalent type of hearing disorder involves *conductive hearing loss* (transmission abnormalities in the middle and external ear). The four principal types of conductive loss are: (1) mixed hearing loss, a conductive hearing loss accompanied by sensory or neural loss in the same ear; (2) functional hearing loss not caused by organic pathology, but attributed to a psycho-emotional problem; (3) central hearing loss, a mysterious ailment caused by a damaged central nervous system, with the patient having difficulty interpreting what is heard; and (4) psychological hearing loss, experienced by sensitive, high-strung singers or communicative, gregarious people who find hearing loss very disabling.

The second most common type of hearing disorder is *sensorineural hearing loss*, which involves damage to the inner ear that leads to a loss of loudness and clarity in hearing. Sensory hearing loss is caused by localized damage in the inner ear, while neural hearing loss (nerve deafness) is caused by damage to the auditory nerve proper. In comparison to conductive hearing loss, sensorineural hearing loss is less receptive to therapy.

In the opening section we alluded to some causes of hearing loss, with an emphasis on noise-induced hearing loss (NIHL) as a chief culprit. Other contributing factors include: (1) congenital disorders that occur at birth or later, such as *otosclerosis*, a correctable malady that onsets in the late 20s-30s; (2) perforated eardrums caused by trauma, such as a single loud noise (explosion) or abusive probing, as when using cotton-tipped swabs; (3) chronic infections and diseases, such as mumps, meningitis, Meniere's disease, tumors, rubella, syphilis, or diseases that occur during pregnancy; and (4) high-dosage overuse of certain medications.

One specific harmful effect of excessive noise on hearing quality is *tinnitus* (various types of ringing sounds in the ears), which may be attributed to a variety of causes, including wax build-up, specific medications, the aging process, or prolonged exposure to high-decibel noise levels. It's not uncommon for singers and instrumentalists to develop various forms of tinnitus, ranging from relatively minor afflictions to full-blown medical problems that require severe curative measures.

Tinnitus becomes a distraction for me only in quiet environments. To avoid this condition in later years, readers are advised to avoid prolonged loud noise and use ear protection whenever needed.

Because singers must often travel by plane, it is easy to acquire *aerotitis*, a common ear disorder caused by air pressure changes in aircraft cabins when changing altitude. Typical symptoms include pain, dizziness, and short-term partial hearing loss, the result of mucous blocking the eustachian tubes and rapid air pressure changes pressing against the eardrum. Symptoms are aggravated when one has a cold or allergy, as inflammation irritates the vocal tract's membranes. Ways to alleviate ear pain include drinking, yawning, gum-chewing, and gentle nose-blowing.

Though singers may not have much control over some causes of hearing disorders, much can be done to prevent serious damage over a lifetime. Here are seven curative measures to observe:

- Avoid childhood diseases that affect hearing, and seek immediate medical attention if a disease is suspected.

- Avoid prolonged high-decibel noise, including loud music.

- Wear ear-protection devices, such as earplugs or earmuffs.

- Keep foreign objects out of the ears and avoid probing, even with cotton-tipped swabs.

- Use ear drops periodically to loosen wax, or have a medical specialist check for and remove impacted wax, perhaps once annually.

- Have a routine medical checkup and audiogram, annually if possible.

- When suffering from a serious upper respiratory ailment, seek medical attention and appropriate treatment.

Most hearing problems can be treated medically, while other problems, such as damage caused by accidents, may require corrective surgery. Some hearing loss can be alleviated by the latest generation of hearing aids, which are small, unobtrusive, and digitally programmed to suit an individual's specific needs. Many singers and voice teachers have found the new hearing aids extremely beneficial in restoring their hearing, thereby improving the quality of their professional and personal lives. Though these high-tech devices can be expensive, some health plans may cover the cost — especially when a job requires extra-sensitive hearing, which is certainly the case for vocal musicians.

Notable Quotes: The Singer as Aural Processor

How has listening to music influenced your singing life?

> The great artist is contemporary, yet also incorporates aspects of his great mentors. We tend to think that everybody lives in isolation, and should live in isolation. There's an absolutely ridiculous notion in voice pedagogy that you shouldn't listen to recordings of singers because, God forbid, you might imitate them! But this isn't a joke; it's the prevalent attitude of probably 80 percent of the voice teachers across the country. — Thomas Hampson

> I was a voracious listener; I still listen to all of my great predecessors. There are a lot of modern vocal pedagogues who don't want their students to listen

to the great singers of the past, which I find really ludicrous. I understand that mimicry is not what we're after, but certainly all great singing starts by emulating great singing. There's no teacher on the face of the earth that can give you everything you need if you don't have a frame of reference.
— Jerry Hadley

Part II
Developing and Executing Vocal Music Skills

Chapter 6

The Singer as Musician

Most vocal experts agree that the most essential qualification for any singer is musicianship — the ability to readily read, learn, and perform music according to a composer's artistic intentions, as indicated by the musical score's printed notation and instructional markings. Whereas singers in past eras may have been able to establish careers based primarily on vocal talent, the contemporary singer is increasingly expected to be a competent musician. The days of having a coach (*répétiteur*) pound out notes until the music is eventually drummed into the singer's head are gradually fading away.

Levels of Vocal Musicianship

The dominant stereotype of singers is that they are weak musicians. But if we survey the professional world of singing we find — contrary to the stereotype — that the majority of active professional singers pursue their art with a high degree of competence. While a large percentage of non-classical singers may lack rigorous musical training, classically trained singers are usually well grounded musically.

The most notable example of a world-class yet somewhat musically challenged classical singer is the incomparable tenor, Luciano Pavarotti, who reportedly has learned a limited number of standard opera roles chiefly by rote, with the assistance of musical coaches and recordings. His equally talented colleague, Plácido Domingo, has performed a variety of standard and contemporary opera roles and has served as an opera conductor with leading opera companies. Not surprisingly, while Pavarotti has enjoyed widespread public adulation, Domingo has received greater overall respect from professional musicians for his superior musicianship.

The good news is that non-classical singers are increasingly demonstrating better musical skills, particularly jazz singers, many of whom have taken music courses or earned music degrees.

Lack of Musical Training in Youth

In contrast to the competent professional, many beginning-level high school and college-age voice students are musically deficient. Possible exceptions include those who have studied a musical instrument for several years, especially piano. Unfortunately, an instrumental background cannot guarantee musical competency. For instance, I've worked with some instrumentalists-turned-singers who have difficulty in producing accurate rhythms and pitches.

Some cases are very puzzling. I've had several students who had studied musical instruments for several years, yet were unpredictably shaky when performing certain rhythmic patterns and pitch intervals. Even after hearing these patterns or intervals demonstrated correctly several times, and repeating them over and over, the students still had difficulty hearing and retaining the corrected renditions. (Incidentally, this problem also appears when some students have problems pronouncing certain words, especially when singing foreign languages.) When faced with such challenges, I usually assume some underlying learning disorder I'm not equipped to handle. On the other hand, when normal students fail to make a correction of a musical mistake, I explain to them that it's probably due to one of two reasons: (1) insufficient concentration and practice; or (2) a learning disability, either real or assumed. I usually leave it to the student to determine which option applies in his or her situation, but I also refer them to experts who might be able to help.

Most musical deficiencies can be traced to the decline of school music education programs. Over the past three decades many music programs have been reduced or eliminated in U.S. schools. Moreover, many existing music programs have placed greater emphasis on rote learning in preparation for public performances, rather than spending time on basic music skills. With the deterioration of public school music education, the responsibility for teaching musical skills has been primarily relegated to the private music sector, and especially to piano teachers. Fortunately, students who take private lessons for several years usually acquire the rudiments of musicianship by the time they enter college as music majors or pursue an independent pop music career.

The lack of adequate musical preparation is most apparent when career-bound music students enter college or university music programs. Generally, the single most frustrating subject for freshmen singers — as well as some instrumentalists — is the required coursework that concentrates on the development of musical skills, that is, music theory, ear training, sight-reading, and keyboard. The inability to comfortably surmount the "musicianship barrier" partially explains the relatively high nationwide dropout rate among freshmen and sophomore music students. On the other hand, those who persevere through the typical two-year music theory program usually develop into competent musicians.

Another reason singers may lack musical skills is that they may begin vocal studies rather late in comparison with their instrumental counterparts. It's not unusual for some students, especially males, to begin vocal studies during high school or the first year of college. In contrast, the typical string player or pianist begins music study in early childhood, when musical skills are more securely wired into the brain and neuromuscular systems.

A Personal History

My personal story illustrates what happens to many singers. Though I'd had church choir experience as an 11-12 year old, I didn't get serious about singing until the tenth grade, when I joined a high school choral group. A benevolent and inspiring director — Alvin Jon "Pop" King — coached me in learning "Mother Machree", which I sang for a tenth grade women's chorus. The enthusiastic response from all those bright-eyed women hooked me on singing, so when "Pop" suggested I take voice lessons from the new voice teacher in town, I enthusiastically agreed. Also, upon Pop's recommendation, during the middle of the year I was transferred to the advanced choral group, and subsequently enjoyed an excellent choral musical experience throughout my high school career that included singing in the school's male quartet as well as performing leading roles in *Down in the Valley* and *Brigadoon*.

Despite this respectable vocal music exposure as a young singer, I nevertheless received no formal music training. My parents offered to provide me with piano lessons at age 12, but I declined since none of my buddies took music lessons. My peer group at that age was more interested in sports than music.

The decision to forego piano study hampered my musical growth, beginning with vocal work in high school, and continuing in college as a freshman voice major struggling to learn music theory, ear-training, and keyboard skills. Indeed, the trouble I experienced trying to master such a wide variety of musical skills in the first few months of college nearly killed my enthusiasm for a music career. Were it not for caring, competent theory teachers and small classes of six to eight students, I might not have survived the first two strenuous years.

I still recall my terror in learning one early keyboard and harmony assignment: "Fairest Lord Jesus", a simple hymn to play, even for a musical klutz. However, because I'd had no keyboard training, I recall spending three agonizing hours learning to play — rather poorly — this simple assignment. The next day in class I was demoralized when it took several blundering, halting moments to complete the assignment. The episode was sufficiently humiliating to discourage my up-till-then ardent love of singing.

I managed to surmount my weak background by learning and performing a wealth of high quality vocal music, some of which was extremely challenging. Yet I can only wonder how my career might have played out had I gained sufficient keyboard skills early on.

So what did I learn from my bumpy ride in basic music skills? Two things. First, whenever possible, take music lessons as a child, preferably piano. Second, if formal study is lacking by young adulthood, it isn't too late to learn, although it may take considerable practice, perseverance, and patience.

The Importance of Musicianship

The most important element of musicianship is having a "musical ear", which is an ability to "hear" — or mentally perceive pitches (either individually or in sequence) — and execute them accurately, preferably after hearing them only once. Many singers, such as Pavarotti, have mastered this skill and are therefore able to function adequately under most performance conditions and circumstances. While vocal musicianship enables singers to learn and synthesize music quickly and securely, some very strong musicians have difficulty with memorization, supposedly because they "get it" too easily. Meanwhile, a weak musician with a good ear might memorize and retain music well, presumably because it's ingrained into the mind-body through numerous repetitions.

In general, a singer with a beautiful voice and adequate musicianship has an edge over a first-rate musician with an average voice. But in the highly competitive world of professional singing, "vocal survivors" are usually well equipped in *all* areas — vocal, musical, dramatic and linguistic. After teaching numerous students with attractive voices but weak musical skills, I'm convinced that although it's possible to develop musicianship in conjunction with vocal study, as happened in my case, basic musical skills should be learned prior to beginning vocal study.

The Components of Good Musicianship

Basic musicianship rests on two main pillars: *rhythm* and *pitch*. Until these pillars are strengthened one cannot be said to have a strong musical foundation. Many voice teachers are puzzled by the obvious inability of some students to grasp certain rhythms or pitches, even after hearing them modeled correctly several times by an accomplished performer.

Rhythm might be considered the most essential of the two basic elements, since it frames and gives directional impetus to a musical composition. Most teachers agree that rhythm can be improved through physical movement exercises, including dance, Dalcroze Eurythmics, and conducting. I attribute my rhythmic skills to many years spent conducting church and school choirs. In lessons, when I've asked students to conduct their songs, I've usually been dismayed to learn they have little or no idea of standard conducting patterns, even though they may have had years of choral experience.

Moreover, when I've asked students to move synchronously and expressively to a song accompaniment, they generally show little physical sense of rhythmic movement, possibly because of shyness or embarrassment. Usually, I must demonstrate what I expect, then urge them to mimic my actions. It's obvious to me that in developing a kinesthetic connection with music, students improve their rhythmic coordination.

Developing a sense of pitch is more elusive, requiring knowledge of intervals and harmonic progressions which can be more easily accessed if one has adequate keyboard training. Understanding harmonic structure greatly enhances the ability to discern pitches in a systematic manner, within the tonal framework of keys and modes. The two principal sight-reading methods involve either the traditional *solfeggio* (do, re, mi, fa, so, la, ti, do) method or numbers (1-2-3-4-5-6-7-8). It doesn't necessarily matter which method one uses, as long as the method facilitates accurate sight-singing technique. The best way to learn how to sight-sing is to concentrate on the task in a regular manner, perhaps starting with simple folk songs and hymns.

After rhythm and pitch, the remaining general aspects of musicianship include:

- dynamic levels (soft, loud, etc.)

- manner of note execution (*staccato* — short, detached; *marcato* — stressed, punched; *legato* — smooth, connected);

- tempo (rate of speed)

- *rubato* (flexible movement within phrases)

- *portamento* (connects notes); and

- embellishment (grace note, trill, turn, etc.)

In addition, *musical style* is a major consideration, especially related to historical periods, composers, national influences, and genre (opera, art song, and so forth). No vocal musician is considered accomplished until a sense of style is evident in his or her performing.

In sum, a consummate singer is a well-rounded musician who exhibits the ability to perform music accurately and expressively, according to a composer's intentions. It is possible for a musically challenged singer to develop an adequate level of musicianship and perform very musically, as Pavarotti demonstrates. However, a vocal musician who is highly skilled at sight-reading and capable of learning a musical score quickly and comprehensively will be rewarded with increased opportunities to master extensive repertoire and wider performance options.

Developing Musical Skills

How does one learn the requisite music skills? Increasingly, excellent instructional materials are being developed to help singers hone their musical skills. For those who need the stimulus and order imposed by formal study in a structured classroom environment, the main option is to enroll in a music fundamentals class, which may be found at community colleges, four-year colleges and universities, as well as some community education programs. For those who are self-motivated and strapped for cash, self-study programs are available through books and web-based instruction. Practical experience and application of music skills can be gained by performing with a choral ensemble, especially small ensembles where each member is required to take his or her turn at leadership. Making music requires a community including both fellow musicians and music consumers, or those who listen to the group's performances.

In closing, I strongly encourage singers to seek opportunities to expand musical skills, first by studying the critical components of musicianship and second, by applying those skills through practice and performance.

Notable Quotes: The Singer as Musician

How do you prepare musically for difficult passages?

> I am a good pianist and this allows me to save a lot of time and energy. I work anywhere, whatever the time, when my colleagues are chasing their coaches with whom they have to sing every day. With my personal preparation at the piano, I can afford to hum at half voice . . . I never solve a difficult [passage] by insisting on it. I have two solutions, which are more mental than vocal. Either I think about it all the time, but silently, waiting to overcome the obstacle directly onstage, when I have no other choice left (it works, most of the time!), or I take advantage of a performance that has nothing to do with it to try

the passage, as a game when I warm up, or during an intermission in my dressing-room. — Plácido Domingo

How did you develop your strong musicianship?

I came by music very honestly and easily: my parents were both high school vocal music teachers and I sang — as far as they were concerned — before I spoke because, as a toddler, I had to sit next to my mother all day long while she gave voice lessons. It's like I had no choice. I was in all kinds of musical productions, in the chorus of this and that; my mother sang a lot of opera and did a Master's Degree while I was a kid. I was never really interested, it was something I had to do, like cleaning my room. I had to take piano and voice and violin lessons, and dance lessons — I had a real stage mother. But it's paid off. — Renée Fleming

Is it important to have keyboard or instrumental skills in developing musicianship?

I can say that having studied piano has been quite helpful. It's not just because I can learn the music alone; that is the smallest advantage. Rather, I think like an instrumentalist. As a piano player, you have to express music without words. When you sing, you have text, of course, but I think you shouldn't count on that, because sometimes the words are repetitive and don't make much sense. The voice alone should tell the story and arouse the emotion, just like an instrument." — Vesselina Kasarova

Chapter 7

The Singer as Vocal Technician

According to Cornelius Reid, technique is the manner in which a physical activity is executed and used to accomplish a desired objective. For singers who possess superior vocal instruments and comprehensive performance skills, respectable success may be achieved without optimal vocal technique, at least to a point. But many singers experience diminished careers because of technical deficiencies, as they may start with a bang but fizzle long before reaching what should be their peak years. My personal experience may serve to illustrate this phenomenon: that the majority of classical and non-classical singers seem content to develop a technical proficiency that falls short of 100 percent vocal efficiency or optimal singing.

True Tenor Confessions

Without question, the most valuable lesson I've learned over time is the necessity of having a dependable vocal technique. Throughout my career I've continuously sought more efficient ways to perform standard lyric tenor repertoire with ease and artistry. I recall a nagging uncertainty during the preparation for challenging performances that centered around such self-questioning as, "What tricks can I use to make it through a particular passage or a difficult vocal work?" Moreover, "How can I keep my voice from giving out?" My technique was so insecure that one teacher teased me about singing with three different voices.

The moment of truth came during the final stages of completing a DM degree at Northwestern University. A one-week, three-stop audition tour to Germany resulted in a contract offer with the Saarbrücken Opera. When the opera management suggested I might be assigned the dramatic tenor role of Calaf in *Turandot* as an addendum to a lyric tenor contract, I was dumbstruck. Already fearful that my technique would not allow me to withstand the rigors of a full-time opera career, I was especially cautious about singing roles beyond the lyric tenor *Fach* (category). So I gave up the promising attractions of a European singing career and high-tailed it back home to the comfort and security of a teaching position at the University of Minnesota. Soon, however, I was performing with all the major music organizations, including the Minnesota Opera and the St. Paul Opera. And though performance success was forthcoming, I was once again reminded that my singing approach needed a major overhaul. I resumed voice study, and now, after more than thirty years of formal voice lessons, believe I'm singing much more efficiently.

My need for extensive voice explorations underscores how important it is for aspiring singers and teachers to develop dependable vocal skills from the beginning. Over the years I've often observed gifted singers who curtail their technical development and inexplicably settle on a technical plateau. This was certainly true in my case, as I had managed to survive for years, thanks to vigorous health, a respectable native talent, gobs of enthusiasm, and determination.

But "getting by" was impeding the maximum development of my ability. The question for any singer is this: Why settle for eighty to ninety percent of your potential, when going for the final ten percent could place you in the upper tier of the profession, where performing and teaching become infinitely more enjoyable and rewarding?

Self Assessment

So, then, how does one know if one's vocal technique is not functionally correct? In general, the inefficient singer experiences labored phonation, with sensations of muscular effort, and the voice may tire quickly. Listeners, upon hearing a singer's performance, may offer minimal or reluctant positive feedback. Singing engagements or awards may not be forthcoming. A technically impaired singer may experience difficulties with completing phrases using normal breath intake, forming a balanced bright-dark tone, negotiating register changes smoothly, staying in tune, sustaining a high *tessitura*, maintaining a steady vibrato rate, producing high or low notes, adjusting dynamics, performing in a legato style, or projecting clear diction. In short, musical, linguistic, and dramatic subtleties are drastically affected by a singer's sub-optimal level of technical facility.

When one's technique is functioning well, the following characteristics prevail:

- Breathing is a normal function, not a super-human effort. Though the breathing system may be taxed under strenuous conditions, as when singing very sustained phrases in high range for long periods, most singing is relatively easy breath-wise.

- Phonation (vocal-fold buzz-tone) is balanced, neither pressed (tight) nor breathy, and resonance is maximized, the result of appropriate vocal tract alignment.

- The vocal tone is balanced between bright and dark characteristics (*chiaroscuro*), and is produced with consistent tonal timbre throughout the entire vocal range, from lowest to highest notes, with chest and head registers appropriately mixed throughout.

- The singer is able to crescendo or decrescendo (increase or decrease) the volume on any single pitch (especially tricky when singing in register transitions, such as E-F# for tenors and sopranos). Loose, flexible, and nimble articulators (jaw, tongue, lips, etc.) facilitate clear diction that sounds natural and speech-like.

These technical characteristics describe *bel canto*, a style of singing originating in seventeenth-century Italy, and culminated in grand opera during the nineteenth century.

Singers are encouraged to conduct regular self-assessments of their voice function, and, when technical deficiencies are noted, take measures to remedy them. I'm constantly amazed at the number of singers who appear content with their current level of development. Some singers may even wonder why they aren't having more success, though to others it's evident their frustration stems from inadequate vocal technique. Though committing to an ongoing self-improvement program requires considerable determination and expert guidance, we owe it to ourselves, our colleagues, our students, and our future audiences to do whatever it takes to become technically proficient singers.

The Vocal Instrument and the Vocal Process

Every musical instrument consists of three essential parts: an actuator, a vibrator, and a resonator. In speech and singing, the *actuator* is the breath that is expelled from the lungs through recoil action. When breath passes through the larynx or *vibrator*, paired vocal folds are set into motion, and the fundamental vocal-fold buzz tone (vibration or oscillation) is then filtered through the vocal tract, a variable *resonator* that combines throat, mouth, and nasal cavities. In addition, the voice has *articulators*, including the jaw, tongue, palate, teeth, and lips. These articulators produce a wide variety of sounds known as *consonants*, and modify the size and shape of the vocal tract to create a complex series of *harmonics* that are perceived as *vowels*.

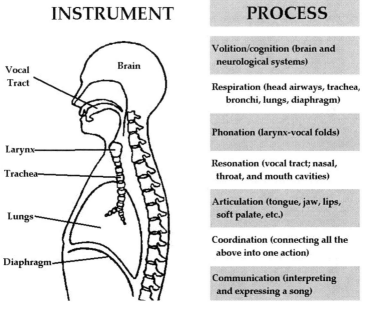

In this chapter we present ten steps for developing vocal proficiency according to the following vocal process:

- *volition* (desire to produce tone and communicate);
- *respiration* (breathing and breath management);
- *phonation* (vocal-fold buzz tone following air flow);
- *resonation* (vocal tract enhancement of fundamental buzz tone);
- *articulation* (forming phonemes to produce words);
- *coordination* (connecting all areas into a single action); and
- *communication* (interpreting and expressing the intent of a song).

This chapter includes illustrations of essential vocal anatomy and some basic exercises associated with each step of the vocal process. Most of these exercises can be found in *Adventures in Singing* (McGraw-Hill, 2004), a textbook/song anthology for beginning-level singers. For more advanced singers, I recommend *Basics of Vocal Pedagogy* (McGraw-Hill, 1998). Please observe that recommended exercises from *Adventures in Singing (AIS)* are noted throughout the chapter within parentheses *(AIS:* Figures x-x, etc.*)*. The website for *Adventures in Singing* includes a fifteen-minute video embracing most of the concepts and techniques suggested here (http://www.mhhe.com/ais3).

Step One: Expand the Mind

- Assess yourself realistically, including talent, background, learning style, and goals (desire to sing).
- Reconcile imagery and reality by learning vocal anatomy, physiology, and function.
- Think positively, creating thoughts and emotions (joy, excitement) that enhance ease of tone production.
- Explore the many dimensions of your voice by producing a variety of sounds combined with body movement and gestures, with a spirit of letting-go, playfulness and spontaneous, non-judgmental expression.

Before you proceed to the mind-expanding exercises, it will help to learn a fundamental exercise called the *lip-buzz* that accomplishes five objectives: (1) consistent breath flow; (2) freedom of the jaw, tongue, and lips; (3) efficient humming; (4) head placement sensations (in the mask); and (5) range extension (see *AIS:* Ex. 6-2).

Some advanced types of mind-expanding exercises are usually included later on in a warm-up routine. However, since our first priority is to set up a proper frame of mind for a positive learning experience with a spirit of playful exploration and experimentation, it may help to explore them at the outset (see *AIS*: Exercises 3-1, 3-2, 3-3, 3-4).

Step Two: Energize the Body (Mind-Body Connection)

- Treat yourself as a "vocal athlete" by giving proper attention to nutrition, exercise, rest, and recreation.

- Improve your physical appearance and body alignment by creating an up-stretched, buoyant stance. Follow the eleven steps listed in *AIS* to establish efficient body alignment (see *AIS*: Ex. 4-6).

General physical-vocal exercises are aimed at loosening up physical and mental tensions, as well as warming up all muscles used in singing. Techniques include stretching exercises and physical movement with random vocal sounds, such as sirens using an "ng" and a "lip buzz" (see *AIS*: Exercises 2-14, 2-15).

Step Three: Develop Breath Control (Respiration)

- Become familiar with the physiology of the breathing system by viewing the illustrations of the breathing mechanism and the air-movement patterns in both inhalation and exhalation (see *AIS*: Figures 5-1, 5-2, 5-3).

When performing breathing exercises, remember to (1) maintain relaxed articulators and a slightly open mouth (avoid clenched teeth), (2) take relaxed, upward-directed, high-arched sniff-like breaths to align the vocal tract for maximum resonance and to provide sufficient air for executing each phrase or exercise, and (3) take in only the amount of breath needed to execute a given phrase effectively (avoid packing in too much breath). Also, when exhaling, imagine "releasing" (not pushing or forcing) breath through a high-arched sniffing channel, with the thought of tone (voice) following "on the breath" (see pp. 91-93).

Basic Anatomy of the Larynx

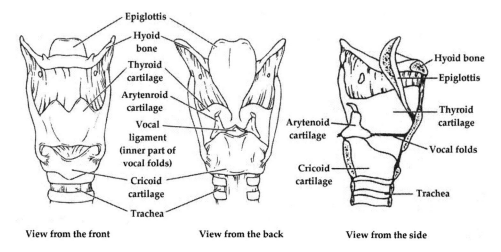

The Larynx Viewed from Above

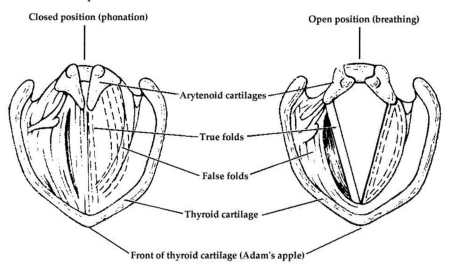

Breathing is the basis of vocal sound, but the emphasis and the ways breathing is taught vary considerably. The two main approaches are the "tone-follows-breath" and "breath-follows-tone" approaches. Striking a balance is appropriate, with attention to both. Most of the selected exercises are accomplished with a minimal amount of vocalized tone (see *AIS*: Exercises 2-16, 5-2, 5-5, 5-7, 5-15).

Step Four: Initiate Tone (Phonation)

- Become familiar with the basic anatomy of the larynx, including the vocal folds.

- Connect breath with tone by learning and demonstrating three types of vocal onsets and sustained phonation: *pressed, breathy,* and *coordinated (balanced).*

Aspirate (Soft) Onset. Whenever one uses an "h" to initiate tone, an aspirate onset results, as when speaking the following: "How are you? He is here; Who are you?; Where is she?" This kind of onset can relax the larynx and encourage easier vocal production. On the negative side, aspirate onset can lead to *breathy phonation.* Avoid this by using an imaginary "h" to encourage an easy-flowing vocal tone.

Glottal (Hard) Onset. The *glottis* is the space between the vocal folds, and a glottal onset is created when breath pressure builds up below strongly adducted vocal folds and explodes them apart. A light glottal onset (hiatus) is normal for clear articulation of many initial vowels, and is especially needed in languages such as English and German. In contrast, Italian and French both minimize the use of *glottal onsets* in sounding vowels. Frequent use of glottal onsets tends to encourage *pressed phonation.*

Coordinated (Balanced) Onset. As in *flow phonation,* balanced onset is an ideal combination of airflow and vocal-fold adduction (closure), which is dependent upon dynamic adjustments between inhalation-exhalation muscles, vocal folds, and resonators. Hearty laughter often illustrates balanced phonation.

- Achieve a coordinated vocal-fold vibration by experimenting with descending-pitch, random-key exercises using a lip buzz, a sigh-glide, a siren sound that uses the nasal consonant "ng" (as in "si<u>ng</u>" and "so<u>ng</u>"), and a moaning or whining sound (see *AIS*: Exercises 2-17, 6-7, 6-10, 2-18).

Step Five: Connect Voice Levels (Registration)

- Become familiar with the three principal registers and their characteristic qualities and functioning: (1) heavy, chest, or low register; (2) light, head, or high register; and (3) mixed or middle register.

- Be able to identify the two major auxiliary registers: (1) *whistle/flute* (high female range, usually above C6, depending on voice type); and (2) *falsetto* (disconnected, hoot-like quality, predominantly produced in the male high-voice range). The high soft voice in male singers is commonly referred to as "head voice," which is a more efficient mixed-registration vocal production.

- Be aware of register changes, or *passage zones* where one register transitions to another. Look for crucial *pivotal notes*, or points when voices suddenly change (flip, crack, break), indicating insufficient coordination. When the voice is coordinated and in balance, the registers connect smoothly with minimal quality changes.

One way to smoothly connect the registers is to slide from low-to-high-to-low pitches using a siren-like tone on sliding pitches (*glissandi*), from low-to-high and high-to-low, without regard for pitches or keys. Use the "lip-buzz" exercise, the "ng" siren, then "ah" or random vowels — particularly the nasty "ae" (as in "quack"), which helps establish efficient vocal-fold adduction (closure) and high-placed mask sensations that promote a ringing, full tone.

The same approaches can also be used when singing other intervals, such as a fifth, an octave, or random pitches. While vocalizing be aware of extraneous tensions in the jaw, tongue, soft palate, neck, and shoulders. Stay loose but energized (see *AIS*: Ex. 7-2).

Step Six: Optimize Tone Quality (Resonation)

- Maximize combined throat, mouth, and head (nasal) cavities to enhance harmonic overtones in achieving *chiaroscuro*, a bright-dark tone quality equally balanced between brilliance and warmth (see *AIS*: Fig. 8-1).

- Become familiar with *tone placement* according to where you hear and sense the predominant tone placement or resonance: *throat* — dark/pressed and dark/throaty; *mouth* — mouthy/breathy and mouthy/pressed; *head* — nasal/breathy and nasal/pressed. Listen for breathy or pressed vocal-fold vibration.

A well-balanced bright-dark tone is the positive result of a coordinated adjustment of all vocal tract resonators in conjunction with the fundamental buzz tone produced by the vocal folds.

As a teaching aid for helping coordinate the full vocal tract for optimal resonance, I've developed the *high-arched inhaling/exhaling gesture*, a technique for countering typical problems of eager voice students who tend to overwork or misuse muscles involved in voice production. Some of these problems occur when students attempt to lift the soft palate, widen the throat, lower the larynx, initiate a buzzy tone, increase breath flow, or articulate text. The high-arched breath/tone concept helps students sing as freely as possible, with a spirit of "letting go" or "release", rather than tightening and pushing to make things happen.

The general idea is to imagine inhaling and releasing

breath/tone through a high-arched pattern that includes the upper breathing channel in the upper part of the vocal tract (nasal cavity). Throughout singing, be aware of sympathetic vibrations experienced around the eyes or facial "mask," in conjunction with a low-breath connection in the abdominal muscles. Also, be careful not to drive, force, or place breath/sound anywhere in the vocal mechanism.

The High-Arched Breath/Tone Release

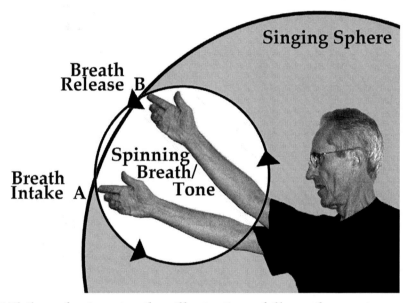

While referring to the illustration, follow these steps:

- Stand tall, buoyant and up-stretched, with a sense of expansion in all directions — up/down, forward/backward, and sideways — within the singing sphere, an imaginary space surrounding the singer at arm's length.

- Extend one arm comfortably forward (point A), with the right hand placed level with your mouth.

- Release the articulators, particularly the jaw and

tongue, and gently hold the chin down with the index finger of your left hand, just to be sure the jaw and tongue are relaxed, and the mouth slightly opened (in a surprised expression mode).

• Take a quiet, sustained sniff-like, "surprise" breath in synchronization with an upward arm movement to position B. (Note: This "gesture of inhalation" or a constant breathing sensation should be maintained throughout singing.)

• Release breath back through the upper breathing/sniffing channel in synchronization with your arm moving back downward to point A in the illustration. (Note: Imagine *releasing* the breath from point B on the singing sphere — as shown in the illustration — rather than *pushing* the breath using abdominal muscles or vocal-fold pressure.)

• Follow all previous instructions, but this time add a vocal tone beginning with an "NG" sliding exercise (pitches 5-4-3-2-1 in keys of F and G); followed by an "AH"; other primary vowels ("AY", "EE", "OH", "OO"); and, finally, short song phrases.

• Imagine throughout singing that breath/tone is flowing in a spinning motion, always releasing and avoiding tendencies to "clutch" or "hold".

Step Seven: Produce Clear Phonemes (Articulation)

• Learn the various speech sounds (*phonemes*) of the International Phonetic Alphabet (IPA), including all primary vowels (closed and open) and problematic consonants used in singing languages, especially English.

• Become familiar with the principal articulating organs (jaw, tongue, lips, cheeks, soft palate) and their function in producing vowels and consonants.

Step Eight: Integrate the Vocal Process (Coordination)

• Aim for a single coordinated *Gestalt* or unified vocal gesture, which, in turn, facilitates artistic expression.

• Be able to distinguish and perform the three basic musical articulations that create contrast and expand the range of dramatic expression: *staccato* — light and detached; *marcato* — heavy and stressed; and *legato* — smooth and connected. Experiment with each of these styles using the phrase "I like to sing" on a 8-5-3-1 descending arpeggio.

• Strive for a full range of vocal expression, including a vibrato pattern of 6-8 pulses per second, the ability to perform with both *coloratura* (agility), *sostenuto* (sustained tones and phrases), *messa di voce* (soft-to-loud-to-soft on a single pitch), a wide vocal range, and a full spectrum of dynamics (see *AIS*: Exercise 10-6).

Step Nine: Perform a Song (Communication)

• Strive to execute all notes and instructions contained in a musical score with accuracy, including pitches, rhythm, tempi, phrasing, and dynamics.

• Research the song or aria's musical and textual background to gain a deeper knowledge of the composer, textual source, and overall stylistic elements to assure thoughtful interpretation and dynamic expression.

• Learn basic English pronunciation, grammar, and vocabulary. In addition (for classical singers), learn the basics of foreign languages such as Italian, German, French, and Spanish, among others. Enunciate all vocal texts accurately and expressively.

• Develop acting skills to communicate better through body language, using expressive posture, movement, gestures, and facial expression.

- Remember that the ultimate artistic goal is to effectively communicate the message of a vocal composition to an audience, according to the intent of both the composer and the textual source, as filtered through your unique interpretative viewpoint, talents, and abilities.

Step Ten: Continue Studying and Improving

Understanding how the voice works is the easy part. Developing your vocal music talent will take much time and effort. It is your responsibility to take the information and to work regularly and systematically with it. Your ultimate success as a singer will result from your faithfulness to the "three P's": *Practice, Persistence, and Patience.*

Notable Quotes: The Singer as Vocal Technician

How did you develop a dependable vocal technique?

> Solidifying my technique took me 10 years. To be a successful singer, one has to start with a natural instrument. But some of us have to really take an enormous amount of time and effort to get the whole mechanism functioning. When I started studying, I couldn't sing high or softly, and I had enormous physical tension. All of these things had to be surmounted in order for the natural voice to come through. It requires time exploring in the practice room. One of the mistakes young singers make is to give teachers too much responsibility for their vocal health and not really try to experiment for themselves. They should try lots of different directions of achieving each goal, because no voice teacher can be all things to all people. You have to gain information from whatever sources you can. I listen to archival and historic recordings. I love watching singers. . . how great singers look when they sing, what their

bodies do, how they breathe, their posture, and their mouth position. I read voraciously all kinds of books on singing, even about the mental aspects of singing, which can often be difficult for people. Curiosity and hard work is what it takes. — Renée Fleming

In my case, six or seven years of studying with the same teacher gave me the foundation. Singing is also a question of the development of the voice, and it involves a set of muscles that must constantly be exercised. It's like an instrument. You have to practice everyday. The voice is more fragile and must be treated gently. I worked every day with my teacher. That's how you acquire a solid technique. You can't become a singer in the space of one year. It takes a long time, you must develop slowly. — Maria Bayo

Chapter 8

The Singer as Linguist

The Role of Language in Singing

Broadly speaking, a linguist is anyone who studies a language with the serious intent to understand and speak it. Professional linguists examine language scientifically, often from a historical/comparative (diachronic) or descriptive/structural (synchronic) viewpoint. Linguists are concerned with the complete system of language sounds or phonemes that may involve sound changes (phonology), inflections and word formation (morphology), sentence structure (syntax), and meaning changes (semantics).

Because singers perform music that is inspired and shaped by language, linguistic knowledge and skills are essential in total artistry. At the beginning of vocal studies, novices tend to concentrate on mastering the sounds of languages, with less attention given to the other aspects. But professionally oriented singers aiming to establish and maintain long-term careers must attain well-rounded linguistic proficiency that encompasses all areas mentioned above.

The centrality of language in communication is readily apparent when one travels in a foreign country. Language ability shapes personal relationships and impacts one's view of life and the world. This is particularly true today, as media, commerce, and tourism are bringing 191 nations of the world into a single global community.

Classical singers in particular depend on language facility to enhance their performance of vocal repertoire, including the major genres of art song, oratorio, and opera. Since their principal objective is to deliver a message in word and tone that stirs people's emotions, singers are expected to be proficient linguists.

In Chapter 7, we noted that musical instruments have three elements in common — an actuator, a vibrator, and a resonator. The human voice adds a fourth element: an articulator, which involves the speech organs in producing a variety of sounds. This highly variable articulating function makes the human voice unique among musical instruments, especially as a means of expressive communication.

The evolution of the speech mechanism, particularly the jaw, mouth (tongue, lips, teeth), and throat (soft palate, larynx), originated with the multipurpose survival functions of breathing, swallowing, and lifting. In brief, the primitive role of the larynx was to keep foreign matter out of the lungs during swallowing and to create thoracic pressure for such actions as lifting, elimination, and childbirth. Over time the vocal mechanism evolved into an instrument capable of producing highly sophisticated speech, giving humans the potential to master several languages.

In contrast to classical singers of the past, singers in the twenty-first century face enormous linguistic challenges.

For instance, consider the typical Italian opera singer in the early eighteenth century. Not only was he or she limited primarily to singing one basic style of music (Italian Baroque), Italian was the only language in which this music was performed! In comparison, today's classical singers must cope with infinitely more complex and challenging linguistic demands.

American classical singers are expected to be proficient in at least four languages — English, Italian, German, and French — in addition to Spanish, which is gradually gaining popularity. American singers may also be expected to learn several other languages, such as Russian, Czech, and Norwegian. Then there's Latin, with both Italian and German pronunciations, depending on a given conductor's preference. It should be noted that all of these languages have common Indo-European roots that stretch back thousands of years, with lineage derived from such ancient tongues as Italic, Celtic, Germanic, Baltic, and Slavic.

Acquiring Foreign Language Proficiency

My personal struggle in acquiring foreign language proficiency began in high school with a year of Latin. In fact, I believe I passed the course primarily on the strength of performing the leading male role in *Theseus and the Minotaur*, a musical skit performed for a Latin Club meeting. Then, taking the easy way out, I opted to repeat a year of Latin in college. Fortunately, I also took a full year of German, which has come in very handy.

The other languages I have learned to pronounce well have been acquired mainly from listening to recordings, from voice coaches, and from having performed lots of repertoire, especially opera roles. In fact, learning a single leading opera role in a foreign language can provide a substantial foundation in learning to pronounce a language (assuming the pronunciation is learned accurately). In retrospect, I wish I had been more diligent in learning certain languages — especially French, Italian, and Spanish.

Of course, the best way to learn a language is to live among native speakers. I've often wondered what direction my vocal career might have taken had I accepted a singing contract back in 1970 and moved to Germany with my family for several years. I'm sure I would have mastered German as a speaker, in addition to absorbing another culture in greater depth.

Although American singers are challenged in gaining linguistic expertise, the scene is even more complicated for the Asian singer, who must learn several Indo-European languages that are markedly different from Asian linguistic roots. In addition, he or she must master English, one of the most complex languages for others to learn. Fortunately, due to increasing exposure to Western culture and languages, rigorous educational standards, and a strong work ethic, Asian singers are proving themselves worthy contenders in the world of singing.

Again, the problem with most American language education is that it begins too late in childhood. Research has shown that development of language skills begins in the womb and peaks in early childhood. People of all ages benefit from sound stimulation that involves body movement, which is essential in developing ear-brain connections. Young children need to be regularly involved in sound-motion activities, as when singing nursery rhymes while rocking, or reading poetry combined with dramatic gestures and movement.

What can be done to encourage language development in early childhood? To begin with, parents and schools should be encouraged to start foreign language instruction as early as possible, preferably before age six, when neural pathways are most receptive to language development. Having playmates that speak another language is also very helpful, as is living in a bilingual home. For example, when conversing with their children individually, a German husband may speak German, and an American wife may speak English. Providing reading and media materials in many languages is another way to give children bilingual experiences.

What about learning languages after age six? It can be done, but the older the child, the longer it takes to establish linguistic neural pathways in the brain. Since language instruction in the American system usually starts in middle school or even later, mastering a foreign language apart from immersion can be very challenging indeed. It's never too late to try, but the learning curve is steeper and the process take considerably more time and effort than it would at a much earlier age. Total immersion, which requires reading, speaking, and thinking in the language, is ideal, but is not always practical for many families in a monolingual culture.

The most popular option for singers who wish to learn a foreign language is to enroll in a course that provides the practice in speaking, reading, writing, and listening requisite to learning the chosen language. Once a working knowledge of the selected language is gained, and once that singer is established on the professional international vocal circuit, his or her ability to understand and speak the language is honed through ongoing practical use and experience.

For a detailed explanation of diction, you may refer to whole chapters in my books, *Adventures in Singing* or *Basics of Vocal Pedagogy*. There you will find charts of vowels and consonants used in major singing languages, as well as exercises for delivering texts with good diction. *Adventures in Singing* also contains phonetic transcriptions of several song texts in Italian, German, French, and Spanish; and the companion CD contains pronunciations of these songs.

The Role of Diction in Singing

Assuming one has a working knowledge of a foreign language and a good understanding of what needs to be communicated, the time comes to concentrate on textual delivery. In singing, diction is the composite rendition of texts according to four interrelated functions:

- *articulation* — action of the articulators (jaw, tongue, lips, etc.) in producing specific phonemes (vowels and consonants, singularly and in combinations)
- *pronunciation* — the proper sounding of phonemes according to standard speech
- *enunciation* — the clear and accurate utterance of phonemes
- *expression* — the full-meaning conveyance of all words and phrases

Diction has a central role in expression, communication, and in rendering an appropriate interpretation. Clearly articulated diction is essential to delivering both the literal and emotional content of a text, including individual words and phrases. When the text of a song is not conveyed or understood, a major piece of the artistic pie is missing, and the audience senses the loss. Beautifully performed music may save a performance, but the intended artistic message may not be fully delivered.

Consider, for example, the typical opera performance sung in English where less than half the diction is understood by an audience. In such cases — and there are many — it's not uncommon to hear opera aficionados complaining during intermissions: "Why don't they provide projected sub-titles so we know what's going on?"

The question "Why is good diction so important in vocal performance?" can be answered with a single word: *communication*. Clear, accurate diction communicates the collective intent of composer, text, and performers to a receptive audience in a manner and style that can be comprehended efficiently and accurately.

While beautiful vocal music can move an audience, the addition of text, which embodies specific meanings and emotions, is a powerful catalyst in artistic communication. Vowels embody, enliven, color, and sustain the emotional properties of tone, and must be recognizable in their purest forms. Consonants contribute energy, structure, precision, and rhythmic vitality to text, making them indispensable to effective communication. In over forty years of teaching singing, very rarely have I had a singer who over-articulated consonants. Rather, I typically find it necessary to exhort singers to exaggerate their articulation of consonants.

The main hurdle to achieving good diction is a lack of efficient vocal production. When a singer's voice is well produced, an appropriate acoustical environment is created for vowel formation, and flexible articulators permit rapid, precision movements for strong-sounding consonants. Though most hypo-functional (lethargic) singers tend toward weak diction, hyper-functional (over-stressed) singers must work hard to overcome excessive tension generated in the articulating organs and throat muscles.

One form of over-stressed diction is associated with "jawing" or "mouthing", which is rather common among enthusiastic young singers, especially in pop and musical theater arenas. The best guide for proper articulation in both speech and singing is that it must appear natural and communicate in a clear, genuine, and expressive manner.

In general, language variants can lead to articulation practices that make singing easier. In an article entitled "Linguistic Variants and Their Effects on the Singing Voice", Paolo Zedda (1998) argues that the aesthetic of a "pure language" must be abandoned, and those who coach singers should offer advice on lyric diction with caution and sensitivity to a singer's vocal production. He stresses the need not for a pure language, but a "comfortable" language that balances the need for intelligibility with vocal freedom.

Zedda says that the baritone Dietrich Fischer-Dieskau, for example, pronounces the German article "der" in various ways, depending on the kind of phonetic space needed for the following vowel, as happens in "der Nacht" (open e) or, "der Liebe" (closed e).

Other barriers to effective diction can be attributed to "foreign accents", including the Americanized treatment of foreign languages, the sins of which are too numerous to list here. In general, however, Americans are more lenient and forgiving of foreign singers who abuse English pronunciation, even offering kind references about their charming accents. For example, the three tenors — Pavarotti, Domingo, and Carreras — have demonstrated in major international public forums how English can be benignly mispronounced yet favorably received.

One amusing story about mispronounced English features an Italian tenor hired by a major U.S. orchestra to sing Handel's *Messiah*. In his opening aria the tenor proudly sang "Comfort ye my people" as "Cahm-for-r-r tee ma-ee peh-oh-pleh", and you can imagine how the rest of the performance went. In contrast, foreigners are not typically as forgiving when American singers mispronounce their language in equal proportion.

What about the International Phonetic Alphabet (IPA) in learning and teaching lyric diction? Thorough familiarity and use of the IPA in studying diction pronunciation can be very helpful. But the IPA is no substitute for the preferred option of intense study and immersion in languages. A major problem in diction occurs when students rely totally on the IPA without any serious effort at learning foreign languages. In that case the IPA becomes a language in itself, devoid of any relationship to natural speech.

Notable Quotes: The Singer as Linguist

How do singers approach language pronunciation and diction?

> Unusual for a singer, bass baritone Thomas Quasthoff shows the same concern for diction as he does for pitch — a testament to years of poetry readings on NDR [German national radio]. Quasthoff's new album of Brahms and Liszt songs is exquisitely articulated, and he has been known to reject new repertoire because, in his view, the words do not match the beauty of the music. — Norman Lebrecht

> I studied in Frankfurt for a year, and one of the greatest aspects of that training was going to the opera three nights a week on a student pass, and I developed my own taste from that experience. I hadn't seen a lot of opera before that. One of the things I discovered is that a beautiful sound, no matter how well produced, without expression and without a sense of text, of meaning, of words, became

very dull to me after about ten or fifteen minutes. I always ask people their opinions, and also people who aren't in the business, and I found in France they're less concerned with correct pronunciation than they are with being able to understand what you're singing. The only coaches I ever work with any more are diction coaches. I believe very strongly in getting the text out. I do think sopranos get a bad rap, in that above the staff it is almost impossible to be understood. Men generally sing where they speak and sopranos do not; I try very hard to be clear but it's virtually impossible. — Renée Fleming

Dawn Upshaw knows some German, French and Italian, but isn't fluent in any of them. Whenever she sings in another language, she works with coaches and native speakers to make sure she gets it right. "Singers take their language very seriously, " she says, but adds with a laugh, "My absolute favorite is English." — Robert Loerzel

Chapter 9

The Singer as Scholar

Rationale for Becoming a Vocal Scholar

A student handbook published by the American Institute of Musical Studies and used in a summer vocal institute held in Graz, Austria, contains a funny but sad story from Leo Slezak (1873-1946), an internationally known tenor who sang for 34 years with the Vienna State Opera.

According to Slezak, opera colleagues played tricks on a good-natured but musically ignorant singer named "Balduin". The first practical joke occurred during a performance of *Armida* by Christoph Willibald Gluck (1714-1787), in which Balduin sang the role of Rinaldo. One evening, following a successful performance, his colleagues introduced him to an old man purporting to be the famous composer Gluck, who was actually impersonated by an actor. Blissfully unaware that Gluck was long dead, Balduin was very enthusiastic over meeting the composer, who in turn expressed great satisfaction with Balduin's rendition of the role. Afterwards Balduin bragged to everyone about having met Gluck, and later on his colleagues had a field day, laughing and poking fun at poor Balduin.

But the practical jokes didn't end there. Sometime later a colleague approached Balduin during a performance of *Pagliacci* by Leoncavallo (1858-1919), saying the composer was sitting in the audience and he wanted to meet Balduin. The tenor, on guard this time, decided to play along. After he was brought to the composer himself, Balduin responded indignantly and triumphantly: "Ha, you can't fool me! You've been dead many years!"

These anecdotes demonstrate how ignorance of music history can harm a singer's reputation and prompt others to label him or her as a "dumb singer". Balduin's lack of historical knowledge may have had little if any impact on his actual performances, but one has to wonder what the singer might have accomplished had he been a better student. A similar question could be posed about Luciano Pavarotti, who has had limited exposure to certain types of vocal repertoire, notably contemporary music and art song. Although there are many other examples of successful singers who have lacked scholarly backgrounds, the reality is that singers on the world stage today need to be diligent in undertaking scholarship related to repertoire they are performing. There is no reason for the "dumb singer" stereotype to continue in the twenty-first century.

Scholarship as Preparation

My own attention to scholarship was rather limited at the early stages of my career, primarily because of ignorance. First as a high school student and later as an undergraduate voice major, I simply was not aware that singers are expected to undertake a detailed study of all vocal music to be performed. For instance, I don't recall having to write program notes for my undergraduate recitals, a task that first became necessary when I prepared my masters recital and subsequent degree and faculty recitals. Nor do I recall any preparation for my first roles in musical theater and opera, other than learning the notes and following the implicit directions of the conductor and the stage director.

By the time I was in graduate school I had begun reading many books on various aspects of singing. It became clear to me that I'd never delved deeply into such areas as musical analysis, historical and stylistic background (eras, composers, poets, and performance practices), word-by-word translations of foreign song texts, authentic pronunciations of foreign languages, interpretation of poetry, or dramatic details. It gradually occurred to me that effective singing actually required loads of careful preparation.

By the time I was working on my doctorate in vocal performance at Northwestern University, I was fully aware of what was expected in terms of scholarship, and from that point on I gave myself to it wholeheartedly.

Tools and Strategies

The vocal scholar's tools range from historical treatises to current technologies, from long-term theoretical studies to daily practical applications. Singers have enormous resources at their disposal, including books and professional journals, multiple editions of traditional compositions, recordings of artists and performances spanning almost a century, and modern technologies, mainly computers and the internet. To make use of these resources, however, one must have excellent reading and writing skills. Though writing skills have been neglected in recent years, they are now enjoying a renaissance, thanks to email and the internet. Perhaps the simplest writing exercise singers can practice is using daily logs/journals to record their goals, activities, and thought processes, providing a springboard for scholarly inquiry.

Strategies for developing scholarship may vary from individual to individual, but there are five common steps applicable to everyone. First, set realistic goals and objectives, such as to investigate all pertinent aspects of a song or aria. Second, schedule sufficient time on a daily basis to research specific musical, vocal, linguistic, historical, or dramatic topics. Third, maintain a written (and recorded) accounting of your research and practice in a notebook. Fourth, seek constructive, objective feedback on your research and performance from others (colleagues and instructors). And, finally, share your information with others through discussion, writing, and performance.

Basic Vocal Scholarship

Basic vocal scholarship is concerned with *all* phases of vocal production and performance — including the vocal instrument, interpretation, and expression — all of which require meticulous research:

• *Voice.* A working knowledge of the vocal mechanism (anatomy, physiology, acoustics), vocal process (coordination of respiration phonation, resonation, and articulation), and techniques that enable efficient voice production significantly enhances mastery of the "king or queen of instruments". Ironically, many competent singers are unable to pronounce or locate significant anatomical parts of their precious instrument, mispronouncing *larynx* as "larnynx" or *pharynx* as "pharnynx" (for example). Moreover, some may actually think it's possible to place one's hands on the diaphragm. Why wouldn't a singer, and especially those who teach singing, desire to have a thorough knowledge of the vocal instrument and its functioning?

• *Music.* Regardless of how beautiful a singer's vocal instrument may be, a comprehensive knowledge of music, including harmonic/tonal structure, form, style, phrasing, and dynamics is a prerequisite for expressive communication. Singers who cannot read music well enough to decipher musical notation must rely on a keyboardist's expertise to drill notes repetitively. A lack of musical skills to execute musical notation of a score — according to a composer's intent — severely hampers career aspirations.

- *Language and Text*. Singers, like competent instrumentalists, should be capable of communicating a full range of emotions and musical expressions solely through vocal and musical means. In contrast to instrumentalists, singers are blessed with music compositions that include texts, which help define and delineate the parameters of musical expression. Though this extra layer of artistic expression requires more effort to learn, the addition of text in the artwork is a boon to both singers and listeners. Moreover, since many vocal music texts are in foreign languages, singers must be proficient at translating texts word-by-word, as well as accurately pronouncing each phoneme according to the accepted rules of speech in the language. The goal in vocal performance practice is to expressively communicate the textual meaning according to the author's intent, in conjunction with the composer's setting or interpretation, which (for better or worse) assumes final authority.

- *Deportment*. Every singer needs to pay careful attention to the way he or she is perceived by others, including physical carriage, dress, grooming, and demeanor. A singer lacking self-confidence and charisma is severely handicapped in performance. And so the ability to see oneself objectively is crucial in developing a commanding stage presence and persona. With modern technology, singers can use audio and visual recordings to assess their performance skills more objectively, seeing themselves from the viewpoint of outside observers.

- **Communication.** The ultimate objective for every performer is to communicate something of meaning and value to an audience. For the singer, communication involves the coordination of many discrete *elements* into a creative yet historically accurate *whole* — in other words, a musical-dramatic interpretation of a vocal composition that expresses the original intent of the composer. Thus effective interpretation typically involves a combination of scholarly research, intuitive insight, and dramatic training, and the desired outcome is depth of expression that communicates a wide range of thoughts, emotions, and behaviors.

Vocal Scholar Role Models

A scholar is a person who has acquired profound knowledge of his or her field through systematic study culminating in mastery. In vocal music an outstanding example of a singer-scholar-teacher is Professor Richard Miller of Oberlin College, who is not only an accomplished performer and teacher, but a scientific researcher who has contributed much to our understanding of the function of the vocal mechanism as director of the Schoepfle Vocal Arts Center.

Richard Miller's publications include *The Structure of Singing* (1986), *Training Tenor Voices* (1993), *The Art of Singing* (1996), *International Schools of Singing Revisited* (1997), and more than 90 journal articles. Vocal scholars do research in order to gather information on composers, movements, and other topics. Here again Professor Miller exemplifies the singer as scholar. For example, one of Miller's recent books, *Singing Schumann: An Interpretive Guide for Performers* (1999) attempts to show why the songs from Robert Schumann's middle and late periods are as great as Schumann's early lieder.

Three international performing artists also have reputations as outstanding vocal scholars. In the ranks of classical singers, Thomas Hampson stands high as a vocal scholar. In an *Opera News* article (January 2001) featuring Hampson, writer Martin Bernheimer calls him "the thinking person's baritone." Writer Freeman Günter refers to Hampson in a *Classical Singer* article (January 2000) a Renaissance man of wide-ranging interests and ideal singer for the twenty-first century. In addition to possessing a first-class baritone instrument, Hampson is a thoughtful actor, a researcher of history, style, and character, and a singer who enjoys recital work as much as performing opera roles.

Another exemplary vocal scholar is soprano Patricia Racette. In a *Classical Singer* profile by Freeman Günter, Racette is called a superb artist who deserves to be called "the thinking person's soprano" (the female counterpart to Thomas Hampson). When asked how she maintains her artistic integrity when music and stage directors have conflicting points of view, Racette replies that though she is always open to any colleague's musical and dramatic opinions, her artistic vision is always strengthened through preparation and research, including listening to reputable recorded performances and researching the opera she's studying at the time. Disregarding historical performance practices, Racette says, is equivalent to "reinventing the wheel every day! It behooves us to know the pitfalls, to know what's been done. It still will be your own."

A third model artist-scholar is tenor Ramón Vargas, who enjoys an international singing career, mostly in opera. In a *Classical Singer* profile, Cristina Necula describes Vargas as a complex and generous artist, an extraordinary individual whose wisdom and knowledge help us grow not only as artists but as human beings. Necula asks Vargas, "How do you manage to be so meticulous, and, at the same time manifest an emotional abandonment that could jeopardize precision, and how do you combine the two?"

Vargas' answer is a strong endorsement of vocal scholarship, as a balance to the emotional expression of performance:

> Going back to the idea of humility before music, if the composers worked so carefully on their operas, we have to respect them. Through our sensibility and talent, we must try to understand and express what they wanted. So, putting heart in it is not enough. It is also important to know much more: the languages, musical styles, history, and so on. True, it takes longer, but when you build an aria or a role in this way, it is rewarding because once you've analyzed it, you understand better what the composer wanted, and you present it in a more authentic way, in favor of the music, without imitating anyone. Thus, you need to find a good balance between these two aspects and be very meticulous when studying.

Scholarship and the Promised Land

Noted historian and author Jacques Barzun (1991) speaks eloquently of the love of learning as fundamental to scholarship, which to his mind is a way of transcending the self. Barzun writes,

> One of the virtues of learning anything is that it takes one out of oneself and into the subject — something independent existing out there, in the world of fact or ideas, or both. To pull the mind back into self-concern and self-excuse is not only a hindrance to learning, it is also a deprivation of the feeling of community with others.

Regarding the necessity of braving the wilderness of discipline and hard work to reach the Promised Land of subject mastery, Barzun reminds us that, "Developing a genuine interest in a subject comes only after some drudgery, and only when the learner gets to the point of seeing its order and continuity, not its intermittent peaks of excitement." The promise of scholarship for the singer is that mastery may finally be attained — after much effort in the trenches.

Singers who wish to become vocal scholars may find a sensible model in the reconciliation of opposites theory, which states that extremes of thought and action are ideally balanced in a central position. Thus, the vocal scholar consistently strives to seek a balance between such opposites as right and left brain, rationalism and emotionalism (head and heart), being and doing, technique and artistry, and so forth. Although one can easily become daunted by such intellectual, emotional, and physical challenges (as Balduin surely must have been), the true vocal scholar is inspired by a sense of purpose and commitment to thoroughly preparing and expressively performing vocal masterpieces, for the benefit of both himself or herself and audiences.

Notable Quotes: The Singer as Scholar

How does scholarship apply in performances of pop songs?

> Dawn Upshaw and her producer at Nonesuch Records, Tommy Krasker, go about their work in an almost scholarly way. Their most recent collaboration, "Dawn Upshaw Sings Vernon Duke," is a good example . . . Some people, fancying themselves purists, object that Upshaw's performances of these pop songs are too pretty, lacking the grit and verve that the material requires. But that's just the point: Duke wrote "I Like the Likes of You" for the Ziegfeld Follies of 1934, and Upshaw's recording recaptures the lilting, goofy charm the tune might have had on its first night out. — Jamie James

What is the relationship of scholarship to effective vocalism, and to expression in performance?

> Ultimately, all that stuff [scholarship] ought to inform what you do as a singer, but it ought not to dominate. We are up there to use our voices as expressive tools to touch people. And I hear so often that so-and-so is a wonderful actress or actor; but if you're doing all that wonderful acting without also singing well, you lose something in the process. It's all a question of finding the right balance. — Jerry Hadley

Chapter 10

The Singer as Communicator

Of the many hats a singer wears, the most important is communicator. While a performer *presents* meanings to an audience, a communicator *transmits* meanings to an audience. All communicators are performers, but not all performers are communicators.

The means of artistic vocal performance can be organized into five principal categories: (1) mind-body connections; (2) musicianship; (3) vocal tone quality and production; (4) language and text; and (5) presentation/communication. The ideal coordinated result is *creative artistry*, a concept that inspires and motivates most performers. Though these topics have been discussed in previous chapters, a summary of each topic seems appropriate.

Mind-Body Connections

The most basic communication during performance occurs when the singer's mind (psycho-emotional self) interacts with his or her body (neuro-muscular self) in a complex chain or loop of interactions. Psycho-emotional activity, on one side, may be viewed as internal proactive impulses that initiate specific tasks; while neuro-muscular actions, on the other side, may be thought of as external reactive responses to various stimuli. For example, when performing a demanding opera role a competent singer executes a multitude of complex mind-body actions efficiently and on cue. However, an external event, such as a glaring scowl or threatening baton cue from a tyrannical conductor, can trigger a sequence of negative mind-body responses that interfere with free-flowing communication. These can be very disturbing and distressing to the performer and, as indicated, may completely upset the communication.

Expressive performance thus requires a constant supply of positive thoughts, constructive self-talk, and creative interpretation of distracting, demanding, or difficult external conditions in eliciting appropriate neuro-muscular responses.

This first level of communication is a process internal to the singer. Effective mind-body communication is created and maintained by a balanced and healthy lifestyle, with attention to factors that impact psycho-emotional and neuro-muscular communication. Some of these factors include a well-balanced diet, sufficient exercise, rest, stress-management techniques; and a spiritual life based on gratitude, compassion, enthusiasm, and optimism.

Musicianship

To effectively communicate the musical and dramatic intent of any vocal composition, a singer must be a competent musician. In addition to proficiency in negotiating pitches, rhythms, tempi, and dynamics, singers should have a solid background in music history (styles), music theory (harmony, counterpoint, form), sight-reading, and basic keyboard skills. Moreover, all acquired skills and knowledge should be applied in preparing vocal repertoire, including an in-depth analysis of individual components such as melody/voice line, harmony, rhythm, and text.

Vocal Tone Quality and Production

Most vocal experts agree that vocal tone quality is the accomplished singer's chief communication tool. Singers endowed with superior vocal instruments tend to be successful, even though other important aspects of their performing artistry may be deficient.

The quintessential example of the "vocal-tone singer" is Luciano Pavarotti, who manages his extraordinary instrument with efficient vocal technique and innate musical-dramatic abilities. The bright/dark quality of his tenor voice and the natural ease of his Italian-style production continue to attract and impress audiences world-wide. Even if Pavarotti were to sing his songs and arias using combinations of vowels or improvised text, he would communicate in the same way all well-trained instrumentalists do — with tone, musicianship, and feeling. For instance, flutist James Galway once gave a profoundly moving performance with the Minnesota Orchestra that culminated in his special rendition of "Danny Boy." There were no words, just beautiful, efficiently produced flute tones performed in a very artistic manner.

Language and Text

Of all instruments, only the human voice is capable of interpreting and expressing the specific meanings contained in song texts of any language. But mastering several languages (Italian, German, French, Spanish, and others) presents a major challenge, especially for the American vocalist who has had minimal exposure to languages other than English.

The singer must not only comprehend the general meaning

of a song text, but also the meaning of every word. A vocal performer's textual delivery is determined by the effectiveness of his or her diction, which includes accurate pronunciation of all phonemes (vowels and consonants), word treatment (inflection, accent, and dynamics), rhythmic treatment (tempi, patterns) and phrasing (emphasis, shape, direction). To this end, reading texts aloud is a highly effective learning procedure. Beginning with a natural, speech-like reading, the singer progresses to a dramatic, exaggerated reading that uses louder dynamics, higher pitches, and more expanded phrasing. I use the term "contouring" to describe a recitation that is very close to singing, whereby pitches, rhythm, tempi, and dynamics are approximated. This is somewhat similar to *Sprechstimme* or *Sprechgesang*, the exaggerated, expressionistic, speech-singing style used by such composers as Arnold Schönberg and Alban Berg.

Communication in Vocal Performance

So far we have discussed communication from the performer's standpoint. Of course vocal communication involves a performer as well as an audience, a medium, and a message in complex interrelationship and synergy.

In vocal performance the "artistic triumvirate" consists of *artworks* (compositions), *performers* (re-creators), and *audiences* (beholders). The "noise" factor might also be added, which include sensory distractions that occur in performance.

Message	Medium	Receiver
Song	Performer	Audience
Composer & Writer	Singer-Actor	Listeners
Creator(s)	Recreator(s)	Recipients

Central to the creative process — and to the artistic triumvirate — is the vocal performer, who is the *re-creator* of any vocal composition. The *singer-actor* is the ideal communicator of vocal repertoire who re-creates in the minds of the audience a believable character or situation in the altered time-space of music-theater.

The process of artistic communication involves the skillful integration of *technique, interpretation,* and *expression*. Each of these terms is explained below.

- *Technique* is associated with the means, process, and manner of *how* any activity is executed. It deals primarily with specifics and mechanics, and operates essentially from left (analytical) brain activity. Without effective technique, it is doubtful that true artistry can be attained.

- *Interpretation* is the act of explaining or clarifying the intent or meaning of a particular artwork — what an artwork is about, in accordance with the creative objectives of the composer, the poet, and the performers.

- *Expression* is the realization of an artwork in a presentation that communicates something of its essence to an audience through a combination of music, text, and drama.

Thus, *artistry* is associated with ends or aesthetic objectives, and answers the *why* question that is illuminated through *expression*. As a concept, artistry relates primarily to principles, and operates primarily from the right (intuitive) brain.

Communication Skills and Modes

According to Wesley Balk (*The Complete Singer-Actor*, 1977), artistic communication depends upon mastering six fundamental skills:

- *energizing* — using psycho-emotional, physical, and vocal energies;

- *concentrating* — visualizing internally and externally;

- *structuring* — varying energy progression to match inherent form and content;

- *imagining* — forming mental concepts of objects, ideas, and emotions;

- *stylizing* — determining the appropriateness of formalized techniques and means according to audience expectations; and

- *coordinating* — synthesizing external/internal performance energies to achieve an integration of opposites.

In *Performing Power* (1985), Balk concludes that the ultimate integration of opposites in the singer-actor involves balancing three projective modes used in performance: *kinesthetic* (body), *hearing/vocal* (voice), and *facial/emotional* (face), each of which must be thoroughly developed. With the exception of the sense-handicapped, almost all persons use more than one modality. However, it is thought that each individual relies on a *dominant mode* for learning and communicating. Because over-reliance on a single mode tends to hinder development of the weaker modes, the singer-actor must conscientiously strengthen the weaker modes, the goal being to create a balance between all three modes.

Effective communication thus depends on the singer-actor's ability to convey the song's message using a full range of sensory information — visual, aural, and kinesthetic. According to Balk, a singer's proficiency in using these three modes can be evaluated using select criteria, and modal over-reliance can be described according to negative and positive characteristics.

Facial-Emotional Mode (Visual)
Negative characteristics: unchanging deadpan qualities; unnatural smiling; lack of emotional expression; hyperactive face (nervousness, darting eyes, tensions, twitches, quivering lips); little communication of mental activity.

Positive characteristics: strongly projective face (both positive and negative) that is easily perceived; facial mobility (as opposed to mugging or indicating); interesting and compelling face; communication of thought processes through face; facial indications of mental visualization processes.

Hearing-Vocal Mode (Auditory)
Negative characteristics: endings of phrases continually cadenced; monotonous or flat phrasing; limited range of pitch inflections; lack of range; glottal tension in emotional delivery; "vocal indicating" (producing emotional voice qualities); artificially produced speaking voice (a pseudo-cultured tone unlike normal speaking voice); similarity of pitch, rhythm, speed, and tone; and extra noises (loud breathing, gasping) resulting from emotional expression.

Positive characteristics: a voice that is unencumbered, lively, flexible (able to change suddenly and easily), interesting and unpredictable, full of tonal variety (color, rhythms, speed, volume, musicality), natural and fresh-sounding, similar to one's speaking voice but with greater energy.

Kinesthetic Mode (Physical)
Negative characteristics: un-energized physical stance; standing with weight on back of heels or one leg; sitting back on the hips; locked knees; shifting of weight from one leg to

the other; excessive finger, hand, arm, shoulder movement (fidgeting); perceptible body tensions; non-performance related movements, actions, or tensions; repeated eyebrow-lifting or forehead-wrinkling; wandering, darting eyes.

Positive characteristics: physical readiness, vitality, energy flow, and alertness; physical balance and centering; physical potential without tension; and easy, quick transitions between physical states.

Some negative traits occur in more than one mode. For instance, excessive facial movements such as eyebrow-lifting, forehead-wrinkling, and wandering or darting eyes may be observed in both kinesthetic and facial-emotional (visual) dominant singers; whereas glottal tension, emotional tone coloring, and excess noises (heavy breathing and gasping) are characteristics that may apply to singers dominant in either hearing-vocal (auditory) or kinesthetic modes.

Identifying one's dominant mode may begin with a simple inventory of behavior, but asking the following questions may also lead to self-discovery. In the following two questions, for example, the order of modes is (a) visual, (b) auditory, and (c) kinesthetic.

> 1. "In expressing emotions do you primarily use (a) facial expressions; (b) voice quality; or (c) body language (gestures, posture, and so forth) to communicate?"
>
> 2. "In your spare time, would you rather (a) watch a movie, watch TV, or read; (b) listen to the radio, attend a concert, or engage in conversation; or (c) participate in some kind of physical activity?"

Emotional Engagement and Enthusiasm

To develop the capacity to communicate the entire spectrum of emotions, the singer-actor must be willing to let go of his or her inhibitions. Such vulnerability requires a risk-tolerant, secure, outgoing and optimistic personality. It has often been noted that singers at the highest levels have these qualities. In fact, we might even argue that the chief characteristic of a charismatic, enthusiastic singer may be his or her deeply-felt passion for singing and the need to inspire a similar degree of enthusiasm and interest in others by means of personal charm or influence.

One such highly charismatic classical performer is the internationally renowned baritone Thomas Hampson, who is frequently quoted throughout this book. It has been said that Hampson possesses:

> A riveting ability to communicate — to be the catalyst in a meaningful intersection of creation, participation, and perception — would appear to be at the heart of Hampson's meteoric success. Nearly legendary is the baritone's ability to reach individuals, including ones basically indifferent to classical song, and draw them in. He can capture attention, turn it into interest, then comprehension, and finally empathy. This is Thomas Hampson's mystery, his *Geheimness* [secret]. (Günter, 2000)

Selecting and Performing Appropriate Repertoire

Since the artwork (or message) communicated by singers is a song, either in its simplest form (folk song) or more elaborate versions (arias), a singer's choice of repertoire is critical. Four principal guidelines may be used in selecting appropriate repertoire.

- ***Musical and textual quality.*** Reaching a consensus regarding quality, value, or worth of any artwork can be difficult, and is often like comparing apples with oranges. For instance, a rock singer's repertoire represents a totally separate category from that of a classical singer. There are ageless, genuine works of art that are widely admired and respected, and there are many works that meet a hasty demise. It's up to the performer to learn the differences in quality by experimenting with a variety of vocal music styles, developing a sense of taste, and deciding what type of music is most suitable and meaningful for a given occasion.

- *Music and voice-type compatibility.* Singers should choose repertoire they can sing effectively, in terms of musicianship, vocalism, and dramatic ability. Yet, for a variety of reasons, many singers make inappropriate selections, including songs intended for other voice types. An acceptable pedagogical practice is to work on challenging repertoire for technical reasons, as long as it's not performed in public (unless it can be performed well). Early burnout is possible for those who push themselves beyond their natural limitations and abilities.

- *Audience type.* It's always a good idea to keep the audience in mind when selecting repertoire. For example, a high school student would be unwise to choose a non-classical vocal piece for a major music school audition. Similarly, a young classical singer auditioning for a musical play or dance band would not be taken seriously performing a foreign-language art song or showy opera aria. It pays to know your audience when selecting repertoire.

- *Music copyright laws.* Most people are aware of the ethics and laws involved when using another person's creative works. In brief, one should avoid photocopying any song or aria that is readily available commercially. Exceptions may be made, for example, when you own a copy of published music and your accompanist needs an extra copy. When in doubt, consult the copyright law (http://www.copyright.gov/).

Performance Anxiety and Coping Strategies

One other condition that may affect a singer's communication is *performance anxiety*, the fight-or-flight syndrome that affects all performers to some degree. Everyone experiences various types of physical or psycho-emotional stress responses in performance situations. These responses include sweating, dry mouth, pounding or palpitating heart, muscle tensions, tremors, gastric problems (nausea, loss of appetite), and loss of concentration (leading to memory lapses). Performance anxiety, or stage fright, can be extremely uncomfortable, and even debilitating, since the energy it takes to sing under such circumstances can make the experience exhausting and demoralizing.

What are some tips for dealing with performance anxiety? The best coping strategy is thorough preparation — musical, vocal, and dramatic — areas completely under a responsible performer's control. Relaxation techniques such as meditation, yoga, biofeedback, and hypnosis can also be explored as ways to calm the mind, improve concentration, reduce stress, and relax muscle tensions. Another effective strategy is *cognitive therapy*, which focuses on the psycho-emotional mechanisms that control and sustain stage fright, including recognizing self-criticism and unpleasant expectations. Finally, in extreme cases, some desperate performers resort to *beta blockers*, controversial drugs that may have negative consequences, especially long term.

Summary and Conclusion

With this chapter we complete our survey of the various skills and challenges singers must master to achieve success in the vocal music field as effective performers and communicators. Developing healthy mind-body connections, solid musicianship, a dependable vocal technique, expertise in languages and literature, and various dramatic skills expands and enhances human awareness, creativity, and expression. Other relevant issues include the relationship between technique and artistry, the importance of selecting and performing appropriate repertoire, and coping strategies for dealing with performance anxiety, a major block for some singers.

When contemplating the wide range of topics covered in our survey, a young singer may be either positively challenged or completely overwhelmed. Though both reactions are understandable, die-hard singers (those determined to become accomplished performers) should not be deterred from pursuing their love of the vocal art. After all, doesn't the intensive, comprehensive training singers receive account, at least partially, for the fact that singers are such interesting, outgoing, and expressive communicators?

Notable Quotes: The Singer as Communicator

Do you think a singer's personality is communicated in his or her singing?

> In my opinion, the quality of a person's singing is not only determined by beauty of timbre, natural talent or an accomplished technique, but also by what he or she carries inside: experiences, beliefs, as well as the cultural, social and emotional background . . . All these elements have an influence on the characteristics of a singer's artistry. I think that singing is the reflection of one's personality, character, feelings, existential concerns. Just by listening, you can tell what a person is going through at that moment, the problems he or she is facing and what he or she is enjoying or discovering in life. In the same way,

every intention is reflected in his or her singing . . .
I have tried to keep this same [child-like] freedom,
spontaneity and honesty in my singing. It is not that
I conceive singing in a romantic way, but I would
never reduce it to such simple elements as sound,
high notes, phrasing or emission. It is all of these
things put together, but there is also what the singer
brings to it from inside himself, from his own artistic
sensibility. — Ramón Vargas

How do you communicate a song to an audience?

A song that lasts only three minutes is still meant to
capture a mood or depict a character. It's like one
of those skating championships — you've got one
chance, and that's it. It's our job as communicators
to paint the picture not just with our voices, but
also physically. The face has to be expressive, the
eyes have to be alive. You have to look like what
you're singing about. It helps bring the piece off the
paper and give it life. If it's no fun, then child, go do
something else. I think you've got to really get a kick
out of it. It has to excite you. It has to move you. And
I'm moved by music. When I get a new piece, I think
'Oh, my God, listen to this music, listen to this poetry.'
That excites me. I love it. — Denyce Graves

How do you "connect" with an audience?

I love actually to see an audience, to bring them
in, to get them right there in the palm of my hand.
That's half the fun of it. We've gotten into the habit,
wherever we perform, of asking for a lighting
rehearsal beforehand, so that there will be enough
light for people to read their programs and at the

same time see my face really well and also Antoine [her accompanist]. — Jennifer Larmore

Should you try to "sell" a song to an audience?

He [Thomas Hampson] thinks that lieder singers should essentially ignore the audience. They should live the story, which invites the audience to eavesdrop, rather than project the story to the audience. "Don't sell the song; let the song sell itself," he said at one point. "Sing. Let the audience come to you." — Ana Kellia Ramares (master class notes)

Part III
Exploring and Enhancing Career Objectives

Chapter 11
The Singer as Amateur or Professional

Three Horses, Three Careers

On the same day in February, three horses are born on adjoining farms in Kentucky. One horse will grow up and be used strictly for pleasure riding on her owner's hobby farm. The second horse will be selected for training in polo and equestrian competition, and later hired out occasionally to weekend equestrians who visit the owner's stable. The third horse will be trained purely as an athlete, and will grow up under the watchful care of an expert trainer, with an eye toward running in the Kentucky Derby and in other major races. All three horses — each of them beautifully endowed and genetically capable of all levels of performance — will live very differently from each other.

Like Kentucky thoroughbreds, singers have at least three career options — amateur, semi-professional, and professional. Though these are not precise categories, they offer a general idea of the career options available to singers. While partly a function of talent, these paths generally reflect the time and effort spent in developing the requisite skills for high-level performance.

Vocal Potential and Career Options

Most humans are endowed with functional voices for basic speech communication, and, depending on their various capacities, practically *all* people are capable of singing — provided they are nurtured in a supportive musical environment. Sadly, many people fall far short of realizing their full vocal potential due to (1) minimal exposure to good music; (2) inadequate music-making opportunities; (3) inappropriate vocal-music training; or (4) lack of encouragement on the part of family, friends, and teachers. This book may never reach thousands of people who are endowed with a beautiful instrument and who for some reason never had a supportive environment.

Lucky is the young person who, as a child, begins to dream of singing in public and actually has ample opportunity to perform in various capacities. Many children do get started quite early, but the dream usually becomes more fixed as they move through high school. That's when my interest began, with voice lessons in the 10th grade. While most students seem to get fired up about singing in their teen years, serious proactive steps usually begin in the freshmen year of college, when music theory, history, and so forth become professionalized. Of course, some pop singers never take any type of formal musical training, though most will have experience on an instrument such as guitar or piano, in addition to experience singing in a school or church choir, etc. The age at which the dream occurs varies considerably — from the young wunderkind to the late bloomer who discovers his or her talent in college — or even later.

As we've indicated, a singer once bitten by the singing bug has three principal options: *amateur, semi-professional,* or *professional*. A young singer may aspire to the professional track and later settle back into the semi-professional or amateur track; such changes in ambition are perfectly acceptable. In fact, going back and forth between these three career tracks is fairly typical for the majority of artist-teachers, particularly for singers who prefer a lifestyle that balances performance opportunities with a stable living situation, which may involve teaching singing.

The Amateur Singer

The most common way of pursuing vocal music is as an amateur singer — as a hobby or avocation. Amateur singers typically exhibit great enthusiasm, and frequently sing at a level of expertise similar to professionals. The amateur's noble credo — "to sing for fun rather than personal glory or financial reward" — strikes a sympathetic chord with every singer. Based on personal observations, some of the happiest, most well-balanced singers are amateurs who enjoy performing as choristers and soloists in local church and community music organizations.

Many former music majors, among them music teachers and professional singers, relinquish professional singing aspirations in order to pursue other objectives. For example, several officers and technicians associated with Make Music Inc. — a Minneapolis corporation known for producing music software — have been music majors who pursue their musical interests on the side.

Two such amateur singers were my mother and father. As a child, I recall hearing them singing folk songs and popular songs, frequently as duets, such as "Let Me Call You Sweetheart" and "The Bullfrog Song". Dad demonstrated a fine tenor voice but his technique was minimal — often strained and unnatural sounding, as though he were imitating what he thought a good singer should sound like. In contrast, soprano Mom sang easily and naturally, but never performed anything demanding enough for me to adequately evaluate her full talent. Nevertheless, it was evident that she had a lovely instrument.

My parents probably had as much or more talent than I have. The only difference was my good fortune in having opportunities to discover and develop my vocal talent, thanks in large part to an excellent educational system and my parents' ongoing support. I'm sure the reader can think of individuals who have attractive voices but who have little or no interest in exploring their talent.

My own amateur status occurred mostly during my student days in high school and college. In my older years I'm returning to that level of performing, as professional paying jobs are typically few and far between for aging singers.

The Semi-Professional Singer

Representing the middle-ground option is the semi-professional singer, who earns a portion of his or her income from singing. Not surprisingly, in order to sustain a comfortable yet modest lifestyle, semi-professionals must also depend on other sources of income, usually from voice teaching, choral or opera directing, or non-music jobs. Private and collegiate vocal music teachers are perfect examples of semi-professionals, possibly representing the largest category of U.S. singers.

In my late college years I became a semi-professional vocal musician, which included part-time church choir directing and singing. I became more of an established semi-professional over the next fifteen or more years as I completed MM and DM degrees in vocal performance, began teaching at the university level (at age 26), and singing as frequently as possible with area opera companies, orchestras, and other music organizations.

A move into teaching may not occur for many professional singers until they have reached their 40s or 50s, depending on various factors, such as diminished career motivation or declining vocalism. Because statistics show that most students graduating with music degrees will most likely teach at some point in their careers, my advice to all young, ambitious singers is to prepare for a teaching career at the outset. Appropriate steps may include earning a music education degree in conjunction with performance, or taking a basic pedagogy course at the undergraduate or graduate level to learn basic terminology, vocal anatomy and physiology, and how the vocal instrument works.

The Professional Singer

The professional singer is one who earns all or most of his or her income from singing. For most singers, serious consideration is first given to a professional music career during high school, when a commitment is made to seek a music degree in higher education. The lifestyles of professional singers run the gamut, anywhere from meager to lavish. While professional singing can be extremely gratifying on personal and artistic levels, it can also present some demanding and stressful challenges.

The closest I ever came to being a professional singer was during my first five years in the Twin Cities of Minnesota, when I frequently performed as a soloist with all of the major music organizations in the area, including the Minnesota Orchestra, St. Paul Chamber Orchestra, Minnesota Opera Company, and the former St. Paul Opera Company. During this time I also served as soloist and section leader at two large local churches with outstanding music programs. I think it's fair to say that I at least approached a professional status for a few years, though I wouldn't consider my modest income at the time sufficient for supporting a family.

Professional Singer Qualifications

So, what does it take to become a professional singer? For the non-classical singer, an academic degree in music is generally not necessary for success. Nevertheless, I hasten to add my enthusiastic support of a liberal arts education for anyone desiring a well-rounded education in preparation for life. A comprehensive knowledge about a wide variety of topics leads to a more profound understanding and appreciation of life, and therefore enhances a singer's level of communication when performing vocal repertoire.

On the other hand, classical singers need as much formal music training as possible, especially if they wish to become artist-teachers. In most cases, a classical singer is typically not ready to consider a professional singing career until completing a graduate degree (MM, DMA), or the equivalent in training and experience. In rare cases, however, some singers may be ready to "go professional" upon completion of a bachelor's (BM) degree.

After completing their academic training program, many talented and ambitious singers will seek entry-level professional training and experience. One option is to participate in an established apprenticeship with a major opera company, most of which are listed in such publications as *Opera America* and *Classical Singer* magazine (see the bibliography). When reaching the critical stage of deciding whether to proceed, postpone, or forego a professional singing career, one should review the requisite qualifications, which include the following:

- *Genetic endowment* — an exceptional voice quality, physical attractiveness, good health, and intelligence.

- *Personal characteristic* — a healthy psycho-emotional state (positive attitude), social skills, ambition, self-motivation, and discipline.

- *Vocal technique* — flexibility and sustaining power, a balanced tone (*chiaroscuro*) throughout one's range, a vocal range appropriate to voice type or *Fach*, and stamina.

- *Musical expertise* — accuracy and ease in negotiating musical elements (pitch, tempo, rhythm, dynamics, and phrasing/articulation), basic keyboard facility, proficiency in harmonic form and analysis, and knowledge of musical/vocal styles.

- *Linguistic expertise* — a basic understanding and accurate pronunciation of major languages (English, Italian, German, and French), clear diction, and a general knowledge of literature (especially poetry).

- *Dramatic skills* — ability to use facial features, gestures, and body language to enhance overall expression.

The most important personal characteristics for singers are *desire, commitment,* and *patience.* In a *Classical Singer* interview (January 2001), the legendary mezzo-soprano Mignon Dunn says, "If you really want to be a singer, there is nothing else for you. Don't do it because you want to do it but because you MUST do it."

Of course there is also the matter of "good luck", or being in the right place at the right time, which in most cases is the by-product of strategic planning. According to the philosopher John Dewey, "Luck, bad if not good, will always be with us. But it has a way of favoring the intelligent and showing its back to the stupid."

The Professional Classical Singer

A profession is an occupation that involves the acquisition of specialized knowledge and skills. As illustrated in the list of qualifications above, classical singing is among the most challenging professions because of the wide-range of expertise that is required. Everyone knows that most professions carry a certain amount of social prestige, and that financial rewards are usually commensurate with the importance of a profession's role within society. To help clarify what it means to be a professional classical singer at the beginning of the twenty-first century, let's look at six basic areas of status associated with professional singers.

Social Status. In our contemporary, pop-oriented culture, commercial or pop vocal music continues to flourish; yet large numbers of aspiring singers are unable to achieve successful vocal careers. And, because classical singing is often considered an elitist enterprise, the situation is even more precarious for aspiring classical singers. Perhaps this viewpoint is a valid one, because classical vocal music (art song, oratorio, opera) typically requires a more sophisticated citizenry to fully understand and appreciate it.

The percentage of the general public supporting classical music is small compared to non-classical commercial music. But participants, patrons, and audiences for classical music tend to increase during stable economic times, as occurred during most of the 1990s. Much of the credit for this documented growth can be attributed to musical organizations giving more attention to (1) programming appropriate repertoire, (2) clever marketing campaigns, and (3) developing educational opportunities, both privately and institutionally. Another major factor may be the positive publicity generated by the so-called "Mozart Effect", which is based on research that gives strong credence to the value of classical musical exposure. Thus both classical and non-classical singers can hold their heads high in celebrating their artistic accomplishments and contributions.

Economic Status. Except for a few superstars, professional singers (pop and classical) in the U.S. are generally not ranked among the highest paid professionals. When taking into account the amount of highly specialized training a classical singer undertakes, the chances of recouping educational costs are lower than can be expected by other highly-trained professionals in such fields as law, medicine, business, and science. On the other hand, singers who establish moderately successful careers can expect to enjoy a modest life style that covers their basic needs, with income to support a small family. The most stable economic situations of all professional singers seem to be those who establish long-term opera careers in Germany, as singers there enjoy health insurance, pensions, and other benefits. Unfortunately, the opera scene in Germany and other countries is not as hospitable for Americans as it has been in decades past.

Political Status. Singers need to pay more attention to the development of political savvy and clout, chiefly, by becoming more involved with issues that influence overall community life on local, regional, and national levels. The typical artistic-type person, including the professional musician, tends to be politically inactive, even though his or her support is greatly needed in lobbying for social, economic, and cultural reforms. For example, U.S. singers who perform with most professional opera, dance, and orchestral organizations are automatically affiliated with the American Guild of Musical Artists (AGMA), a union formed to protect the professional interests of singers, dancers, and instrumentalists. Yet, the record shows that most singers fail to participate in the governing of their profession, opting instead to relegate most governing to a few colleagues who serve as their representatives.

Personal Status. As a professional group, singers tend to be morally sound, socially adept, and aesthetically sensitive to the finer aspects of life. Partly due to their comprehensive training as performers, they tend to be outgoing, positive, and generous in their personal relationships. However, the inordinate attention they give to self-improvement issues can create strong egos that strain relationships, especially during the early-career stage. The lonely gypsy-like lifestyle of the typical U.S. singer also tends to exacerbate the problem of building lasting relationships, particularly with loved ones. For instance, while traveling all over the globe it can be very difficult to sustain a close, loving relationship with one's partner, spouse, or children. Coping with loneliness, variable living conditions, changeable circumstances, and an unstable home environment can be very stressful on one's psyche. But despite the difficulties imposed by the typical professional singer's lifestyle, it seems possible to achieve a balance between singing career and personal life.

Artistic Status. It is in the capacity of artist that professional classical singers discover their true *raison d'etre*, or purpose. As "re-creators", singers must be very adept at interpreting, expressing, and communicating the psycho-emotional content of each vocal composition, according to the original intentions of the creators (textual source and composer). Because singers rarely perform alone, the ability to collaborate effectively with others is extremely valuable. Dependability, trustworthiness, honesty, optimism, positive attitude, and a good sense of humor are essential in helping create exciting, memorable performances. Becoming a true artist requires giving serious, in-depth attention to mastering all of the qualifications listed earlier.

Role-Model Status. When singers secure their careers and achieve respectable reputations, the status of "role model" is automatically bestowed, placing them on public display for all to view, criticize, admire, and emulate. Young aspiring singers in particular look to the most exemplary singers for inspiration, instruction, and guidance. And it is in this arena that professional singers have their greatest influence on the future of vocal music, by modeling appropriate behavior in their personal, social, and artistic lives. Singers who exemplify well-balanced lives, such as Frederica von Stade, Dawn Upshaw, and Mark Delavan, provide the type of role models needed in our noble profession. Each of these singers will probably agree with Germaine Greer, who reminds us that "careers are a poor substitute for a life".

Future of the Professional Classical Singer

The future of the vocal artist continues to be a hotly debated topic. Some reports are discouraging, including sporadic news announcing significant decreases in government funding for the arts. Another prominent issue is the ongoing legal battle concerning the infringement of copyright laws associated with recorded and printed materials created by musicians, as exemplified by the public's wholesale copying of music located on internet websites. On the other hand, there are some signs that art and artists will continue to fare well. For example, in recent years data collected by premiere organizations such as Opera America and the Metropolitan Opera Guild indicate gradual growth in the amount and frequency of opera performances. Moreover, professional musical theater touring companies are displaying a growing vitality, both nationally and internationally.

During economic downturns such positive trends may slow down or reverse. This occurred, for example, in 2002. Moreover, solo opportunities in recital and with orchestras and choral groups appear to be waning, especially when comparing the ratio of performances to singers. The main problem seems to be too many singers chasing a limited number of singing positions, and it comes as no surprise that the ubiquitous lyric soprano has the hardest time competing.

On the local level, singing opportunities for trained singers include religious, entertainment, and commercial music. *Religious music* includes solo work as a church or synagogue soloist for regular worship services, weddings, and funerals. *Entertainment music* is associated with special events, such as conventions and sports events (national anthem). *Commercial music* deals primarily with the media, including television, radio, and the internet. Increasingly, both the church scene and the entertainment industry tend to favor pop musicians. To cope with this tendency, many classical singers are developing hybrid techniques that allow them to switch back and forth. The outcome is uncertain, with many "gatekeeper" pedagogues decrying the invasive pop culture, and bemoaning the eventual demise of classical singing.

Another potentially negative development is the increase in electronically amplified performances, especially in opera. No one can predict the outcome of the electronic revolution in music, including the promotional potential of the internet, or the capability of recording technology to alter and synthesize the human voice. Digital technology will continue to revolutionize the recording, editing, and transmission of vocal music, just as it has every other art form.

Despite all of the negative possibilities, one thing is certain. Since the arts serve as vehicles of expression for the emotional and aesthetic needs of the human community, vocal artists will always have a vital role to play in society.

To paraphrase the words of Martha Graham: "No artist is ahead of his time. He (she) is his time. It is just that the others are behind the time."

Notable Quotes: The Singer as Amateur or Professional

How did you get started as a professional singer?

> I've been training all my life: I started in church, where I had fantastic choir directors. Choir was a really important thing in my life. I had one of the best basic musical educations you could get. — Jennifer Larmore

What does it take to become a professional singer?

> My advice to a young colleague at the beginning of his or her career: First, be realistic and coolly estimate your capabilities: do you want to sing at parties to delight your family and friends, or do you feel you have what it takes to undertake a singing career (I don't even speak of an international career, just of becoming a professional singer). Second, work hard to strengthen your natural skills. Acquire a solid education, which means much more than mere musical training. You must cultivate yourself in the most extensive sense of the word; deeply and, also, on time! Third, when you begin your career, learn to say "no". Resist proposals that may be very tempting but premature, that is, roles that are not convenient for you to sing (yet). — Ramón Vargas

What is the best path to a future vocal career?

> I think that as a young singer, you have to be very protective of yourself. It is very easy to get distracted by outside influences, by all the things that need to get done, and you can forget the meditative side of your life . . . I do not believe there is a path or set of answers that guarantee even a shot at fulfillment

or success. I do know a few things that are non-negotiable: if you are going to have a career, you must sing well and have a built-in voice saying: 'Don't do this now, because it will shorten your career.'
— Thomas Hampson

Chapter 12

The Singer as Business Manager

Rationale for Developing Business Expertise

Aspiring singers tend to downplay economic concerns in the early stages of their career, when their primary focus is developing performance skills. Yet money is essential to sustaining artistic aspirations — a superior vocal music talent does not guarantee regular engagements or steady income.

How does an upwardly-ambitious singer maximize earning potential, manage personal business matters, and develop a comfortable and rewarding lifestyle? Ten steps in this chapter are designed to help the singer plan, assess, develop, market, package, and sell his or her art form.

Every successful business venture is firmly founded on a set of beliefs, principles, goals, and objectives that require positive, constructive action to be fully realized. Taken into account are available resources, the market need of any product or service, and an honest appraisal of any strengths and weaknesses that deal with the "who, what, why, how, and when" aspects of any serious undertaking. In developing a viable singing career, it is necessary to establish clear-cut goals and objectives, from short-term to long-term.

> **Step One.** Write out a general mission statement that summarizes in a single paragraph who you are and what you wish to accomplish, in conjunction with a game plan according to short, medium, and long-range objectives. Remain flexible, periodically revising your mission statement, goals, and objectives as you continue to develop your talent.

Product Quality

In both business and singing a mediocre product will not earn the enthusiastic support of the sales force (teachers, coaches, managers, conductors, directors), and most certainly will be ignored by the general public (audience). Only first-rate vocal products survive the highly competitive music market, and only meager financial rewards will be forthcoming for those whose product is under par. Relatively few singers — both classical and non-classical — earn comfortable incomes. The rare exceptions are vocal superstars and savvy niche performers, for example young singers such as Charlotte Church and Britney Spears.

> **Step Two.** Develop your talents to the fullest — vocally, musically, linguistically, dramatically, and expressively; give equal attention to developing interactive people skills, including the ability to write well.

Product Reliability

A product of high quality usually meets reliability standards, notably in terms of sturdiness and stamina. A singer achieves similar reliability qualifications by developing a strong physical constitution based on a long-term, regular physical regime that includes proper diet, exercise, rest, and recreational pursuits. Psycho-emotionally, the singer must also demonstrate the kinds of positive attributes that assure reliability, such as conscientiousness, self-motivation, and commitment. Singers who exemplify good mind-body health and self-discipline will rarely miss, cancel, or be late for rehearsals and performances.

> **Step Three.** Make mind-body health a top priority by eating well, exercising regularly, getting plenty of rest and recreation; also, be sure to secure basic health insurance coverage.

Product Packaging

Strongly related in importance to product quality and reliability is design (attractiveness), or "packaging". When faced with a multitude of choices, the average consumer is naturally drawn to the most interesting and appealing products. Similarly, a talented but physically unattractive singer (due to personal neglect) may suffer a profound competitive disadvantage. There is a growing trend among youth to over-eat and under-exercise, creating a generation of potentially unhealthy, unattractive singers. Sadly, there's a truth to the popular saying "the opera isn't over until the fat lady sings", portending a potentially unpleasant scenario for singers of the twenty-first century.

> **Step Four.** Give serious attention to "packaging" — overall physical appearance, grooming (moderate makeup and hairstyles for classical singers) and attire appropriate for all professional activities, especially auditions, rehearsals and concerts.

Market Niche

Competition in any market can be fierce, and particularly daunting in the vocal arena. Most products that manage to survive fit a peculiar niche in a specific market area, one in which there is minimal competition, or where a special product demonstrates superior quality and reliability.

One major problem for most ambitious, talented classical singers is that the vocal marketplace provides neither sufficient opportunity nor adequate compensation. The shortage of opportunities makes it difficult for some singers to specialize and excel in their preferred areas of expertise. For example, a singer who loves to perform art song recitals will not find many outlets. Even rare voice types, such as a gifted counter-tenor, may struggle with securing singing engagements, primarily because their highly specialized repertoire is limited. Opera singers may find it easier to specialize in more lucrative niches. Examples of these niches include the dramatic coloratura engaged to regularly perform the Queen of the Night (in Mozart's *Magic Flute*) in various European opera houses, or the more dramatic voice types destined for certain Wagner and Verdi roles. On the other hand, versatility may actually provide a special niche for quick learners who can effectively negotiate wide-ranging repertoire, including a variety of opera and oratorio roles, in addition to performing art-song recitals.

> **Step Five.** Actively seek and receive objective, realistic assessments of your vocal strengths and weaknesses from vocal experts, colleagues, friends, and family (in that order). Then, determine what you do best and what you wish to accomplish in your singing career, and commit wholeheartedly to pursuing it.

Financial Support

Many worthy products fail from lack of a firm financial base; first, in covering expensive start-up costs; and, second, in earning ongoing income to develop, promote, and secure the product's market niche. A singer's continuing education during the career-building stage can be very expensive, and discouraging because of the hardships involved in repaying large educational loans. Unlike students pursuing more lucrative professions — engineers, medical doctors, research scientists, and business majors — singers may incur heavy debts and spend many years recovering financially. When a singer makes the crucial decision to initiate a singing career, investment capital is needed to promote and package the artistic product.

In the early years, the young singer must find ways to support his or her "vocal habit" with a life-sustaining income. The ideal strategy is to find a flexible part-time job that pays well, for example, positions that require expertise with computers and technology. Jobs that diminish one's energies and vocal powers, such as working in polluted environments, telemarketing, or teaching K-12, should be avoided. On the other hand, certain regular singing engagements, such as professional solo/section leader positions with church choirs or synagogues, may fulfill several needs: steady income, social support, minimal interference with career objectives. Singing in community, opera, and musical theater choruses may also provide professional experience, educational opportunities, and income. However, unless the terms are exceptional, singers should be cautious when accepting long-term engagements with choral and opera organizations that feature irregular scheduling and require heavy time commitments.

> **Step Six.** Develop a modest lifestyle and manage money carefully. Avoid extravagant purchases and shop in thrift stores for clothing and home furnishings. Set aside 5 to 10 percent of your earnings for savings and investments in an emergency or rainy-day fund.

Product Marketing

No matter how worthwhile and attractive a product may be, it can languish in obscurity without effective publicity and marketing. Similarly, a singer who fails to develop a systematic marketing plan, network with colleagues, and maintain a continual barrage of publicity coverage, will remain unknown or, in cases where recognition has been achieved, fade from the professional scene.

Unless professional management is secured, most singers must assume responsibility for managing their own careers, including creating and distributing publicity materials. The singer-business manager begins by developing a realistic game plan for accomplishing career objectives, based on short, medium, and long-term goals. Individual plans will of course vary considerably, according to a person's age, training, experience, and family status.

For instance, a 22-year-old unmarried singer who wants to attend graduate school is more aware of short and medium range plans as determined by the number of academic terms required to earn graduate degrees, from two years (for a masters degree) to five years (for a doctorate). In contrast, a 28-year-old married singer, who has a child and is completing a graduate degree, will have a much different career horizon. In any case, the individual singer must determine general and specific strategies for accomplishing personal objectives, using inexpensive self-promotion strategies whenever possible. Since this aspect of business management requires considerable action, several steps are needed to cover all areas of concern.

> **Step Seven.** Create a comprehensive publicity packet that comprises a variety of materials, including:
> - an attractive, one-page résumé on top-quality white

paper (two pages at most) that lists personal data, educational training (schools, degrees, teachers), performing experience (opera, oratorio, recital), honors (contests) and work experience (what, when, and where);

- a 5" by 7" black-and-white "real-you" photograph (for inexpensive duplicates, check out ABC Pictures — 888-526-5336);

- an optional one-page, two-sided, 8" by 11", simple, inexpensive, and attractive brochure that includes a photo and an outline of résumé-style information;

- at least one general, all-purpose CD recording that represents appropriate repertoire for the type of engagements you're seeking, or one or two CD recordings aimed at specific niches (for inexpensive CD duplications, check out DPS Video — 716-835-4620);

- a video tape (for certain artists, such as dancers, pop singers, musical theater singers) that demonstrates requisite performance skills (singing, dancing, acting); and

- a simple, attractive personal website that includes the information contained in your résumé and/or brochure, one or two photos, and any pertinent supplemental information, with appropriate links to other websites (check out http://www.classicalconcepts.com for more information).

Step Eight. Take advantage of all opportunities to publicize and demonstrate your credentials in the vocal marketplace, including:

- listing your name in on-line singer directories, for example, the website search list provided by *Classical Singer* magazine (www.classicalsinger.com);

- compiling a list of appropriate musical organizations to contact (check out musicalamerica.com), preferably those ranked less than C (A and B organizations are for experienced singers);

- compiling an email list of colleagues, institutions, music organizations, etc., and discreetly using such information for most professional correspondence; and

- participating in appropriate vocal competitions and auditions (when thoroughly prepared and healthy; avoid auditioning when ill or in bad voice).

Step Nine. When you have sufficient experience in performing, preferably including traditional opera roles with reputable companies, consider contacting professional management. This may require moving to New York City (or perhaps Europe for opera careers) or another metropolitan area, in order to be near the action. At this stage, a compatible, supportive agent (a younger, booking type) or manager (an older, mentor type) should be of great help in accelerating your career.

Appreciating, Assessing, and Sustaining Your Product

To remain competitive, all products need a regular, rigorous evaluation, including feedback from all sources — company personnel, niche competitors, retailers, and the general public. Likewise, vocal products need ongoing assessment and improvement.

Once a singer has made every attempt to perfect his or her craft and market it effectively, the principal challenge is to maintain a positive perspective, which includes a sense of self-worth and commitment to one's personal life mission. If one stays true to the course and abides by guidelines that promote a balanced life, financial considerations usually fall into place.

Step Ten. After tending to the first nine steps, focus attention on psycho-emotional issues, including:

- appreciating your talent and continuing to develop it with self-motivated, ongoing learning;

- assessing your talent regularly by listening to and/or viewing recordings of your practices and performances, and by soliciting feedback from respected experts;

- maintaining a balanced, realistic perspective about yourself and your talent; and

- remaining patient regarding the pace of your career, and open to any promising opportunities.

The chief lesson in the ten steps is that artistry has a better chance of flourishing when supported with effective business skills. Willa Cather observed that "religion and art spring from the same root and are close kin, but economics and art are strangers." Singers must counter this observation with business skills that will allow them to freely pursue their art — with enthusiasm, security, and ease.

Notable Quotes: The Singer as Business Manager

What non-vocal skills help build a singing career?

> A career-life is made through discovering the conditions, both professional and personal, that you must navigate in order to realize artistic opportunities. This process requires a different set of skills than those demanded by the artistic process. Skills like networking, writing, public speaking, self-reliance, strategic planning, entrepreneurship, fundraising, financial planning, teaching, and community partnering are some of them. Some skills overlap, such as discipline and creativity, which can carry you

far in your career. But without broad career skills, your prospects in the performing arts will be limited.
— Derek Mithaug, The Juilliard School

A musician today needs to be a small-business person and build a career that way. Managers don't take young potential talents under their wings and develop them the way they used to do. It's up to the musician now to get the work, to decide what the head shot should look like, to write the bio. Competition has driven the level of musicianship up. What sets you apart now is business savvy. — John Blanchard, Manhattan School of Music

Is networking an important consideration in a singing career?

Employers and job-seekers alike affirm that networking is the most powerful tool you can use to find a job or internship. Networking puts you in touch with people who have the ability to (1) provide insights about a career field, employers and their needs, and realities of employment beyond what you learn in the classroom or from printed resources; (2) refer you to other people who can be helpful; and (3) ideally, connect you with information about a job or internship opportunity. Up to 75 percent or more opportunities never get listed anywhere but are filled by candidates who were known by the employer, often through networking contacts. Networking is about getting information that can help you with your search. Networking is a cumulative process, like making a friend — sometimes a friendship isn't established in just one contact. Typically, one piece of information leads to another piece of information and so on. — Wendy Miller, Oberlin College

Chapter 13

The Singer as Pedagogue

To Teach or Not to Teach

There is an old dictum: those who can sing, do, and those who can't, teach. Though this bitter saying may have derived from anecdotal observations, it certainly doesn't apply across the board to all voice teachers. The saying should be reworded to reflect positively on teaching: Those who can teach, do, and those who can't, sing. Or, to avoid bashing altogether: "Those Who Can, TEACH", as Marney K. Makridakis puts it in the title of an article in *Classical Singer* (September 2002).

A negative perception of teaching persists to some extent in academic institutions world wide, where most vocal music training occurs. Indeed, former professional singers who teach in colleges and universities may prefer to be thought of as of resident artists rather than pedagogues, even though their major responsibility is teaching.

A similar attitude prevails among vocal performance students, particularly at the undergraduate and masters degree levels. While aspiring professional singers under 30 are understandably unenthusiastic about teaching, older students pursuing DMA degrees in vocal performance typically reconcile themselves to becoming teachers, if only to enhance future employment prospects. Older students, who have had time to weigh the realities of singing and teaching, make the transition to a voice-teaching career more easily.

I did not consciously entertain the idea of becoming a voice teacher until I realized I was becoming one. This occurred during my freshman year in college when I served as a church choir director. At that point I wasn't much concerned with the direction of my career, as long as I had opportunities to perform. Fortunately, I was very active at the time, conducting and singing as much as possible.

My exposure to expanded teaching began with my first full-time position as a Director of Music and Youth Programs in a moderate-sized Methodist Church, where I used teaching skills in working with choristers. At that time my long-term goal was to become a Minister of Music in a large church where I could develop a first-rate music program that included several choirs, ranging from children to adults.

After two years in the full-time church position, I undertook a masters degree program in vocal performance at the University of Southern Mississippi, where Dr. David Foltz, choral director and chair of the music department, encouraged me to explore music education and voice teaching. Upon graduation I acted on his sage advice by accepting a position as choral director at a large high school in Jackson, Mississippi, where there was a strong music tradition with first-class choral, band, and music theater programs. All the while I was singing as frequently as possible, including my professional opera debut with the Jackson Opera Guild singing the role of Lt. Pinkerton in Puccini's *Madame Butterfly*. I also began giving private voice lessons to high school students during the summers before and after my year of high school teaching.

After that single year of high school teaching, I was invited back to the University of Southern Mississippi to serve as a voice teacher and assistant choral director. During a six-year tenure there I gained valuable experience as an applied voice teacher. In 1969 my family and I moved to Evanston, Illinois where I completed a DM degree in vocal performance at Northwestern University. Upon graduation we transplanted ourselves once again in 1970 to Minneapolis, where since then I've taught voice and pedagogy courses at the University of Minnesota's School of Music. That's the story of how I became a young pedagogue. It was not an intentional goal, but simply evolved. Though I've had occasional thoughts of becoming a professional singer, I've truly enjoyed the combined professional life of teaching and singing, which I balanced equally through my late 20s and mid 30s. Over the past three decades I've gradually become more of a teacher than a performer, a typical career pattern for aging singers.

The What, Who, and Why of Pedagogy

What is pedagogy and who is a pedagogue? *Pedagogy* may be defined as the science, art, and profession of teaching based on principles and methods that facilitate systematic learning. A *pedagogue* is simply one who teaches. *Voice pedagogy*, a term commonly used in academia when speaking of voice teaching, has been defined as "the aggregate of principles, rules, and procedures pertaining to the development, exercise, and practice of the art of singing; and process of training, by a prescribed course of study or technical discipline" (Fields 1947). In sum, vocal pedagogy helps singers develop into skillful and expressive performers, by means of information and practice, in a manner that is comprehensive and methodical yet creative and flexible.

"Why should singers develop teaching skills?" is often asked by young singers. Studies show that approximately 95 percent of all music majors will teach at some point during their careers. Of course, 100 percent of music majors will teach at least one student: himself or herself! This fact alone supports the main rationale for pedagogical training: to teach oneself effectively, both when formal voice study is not possible and when studying under a teacher's supervision. Formal study typically consists of one weekly voice lesson of 30 to 60 minutes in length, plus six to ten hours per week in isolated self-learning. Though certain teaching aids may be used, such as audio and video tape recorders, mirrors, and acoustical biofeedback equipment, the student working alone (in self-teaching) must be able to interpret results, make diagnoses, and decide effective solutions.

Practically everything a teacher is expected to master applies directly in self-teaching. For example, a comprehensive vocal pedagogy course will cover a wide range of pertinent topics, including the following:

- philosophy and psychology of singing (origins, purpose, benefits);
- mind-body connections (general mind-body health, vocal athleticism, speech-to- singing);
- an overview of the vocal process including the anatomy and physiology of respiration, phonation, registration, resonation, articulation, coordination;
- vocal health and care (disorders and cures);
- vocal performance skills (song study, repertoire selection, diction, body language, performance anxiety,

dramatic interpretation and expression); and

- information about teaching (history of singing and pedagogy, learning/teaching modes, foundations, tools, strategies, business matters).

Another benefit of learning to teach is that the experience gained in observing and instructing other singers exerts a powerful influence on one's own performance skills. Vocal pedagogy students frequently report that explaining and demonstrating a concept or exercise to someone actually helps clarify and reinforce it for themselves. I know that teaching has greatly influenced my vocal development, just as ongoing vocal study and performance has informed my teaching. It's been my experience that the learning-teaching feedback loop becomes richer, more secure, and more creative as one strikes a dynamic balance between singing and teaching.

Voice Teaching as a Career Option

What about teaching as a career choice for singers? The strongest rationale for considering an artist-teacher career is the documented growth of employment opportunities for singers as teachers in elementary and secondary schools and in institutions of higher education. Many singers prefer the balanced singer-teacher lifestyle in comparison to the typical professional singer's lifestyle, which generally offers less financial security and stability. The benefits of teaching are impressive, including:

- a career focused on vocal music, a rigorous discipline requiring encyclopedic knowledge and comprehensive skills in a variety of areas including vocal technique, song repertoire, languages, music theory and analysis, literature and poetry, keyboard playing, music history, drama, and performance;

- the cultural significance of vocal music, a valued resource based on the human voice as an instrument for effective and expressive communication in speech and singing;

- intangible rewards in guiding others toward the attainment of worthwhile goals, both educational and personal;

- a balanced lifestyle that permits some degree of financial security and family stability;

- a respectable social status due to a high level of respect and influence in the community; and

- the self-improvement that results from ongoing mastery of knowledge and skills that exercise all of one's intellectual and physical resources.

If you are interested in exploring the possibilities of teaching, here are some steps you can take to get you started:

- Begin by reading some recommended pedagogy books (see bibliography).

- Observe a few successful, experienced teachers giving lessons to male and female students, following their progress over a period of several weeks.

- Take a voice pedagogy course. Though courses vary greatly in approach and subject matter, enrolling in one may be very helpful — especially if it provides an opportunity to teach one or two students under the supervision of the course instructor.

- After gaining pedagogical knowledge and skills, consider taking a practicum course that involves teaching one or two students under the supervision of an experienced teacher.

- Following the practicum training, you might seek a

supervised apprentice teaching program, possibly in connection with a high school vocal music program.

• Finally, there are plenty of opportunities to gain teaching experience, including developing a home-based private studio or making arrangements with music directors in churches or schools to teach on a part-time basis.

Drawbacks to Teaching

It should be pointed out that there are some minor drawbacks to being a vocal pedagogue:

• Heavy teaching schedules filled with a variety of students bringing wide ranges of talent and motivation, some of whom are invigorating to teach but others who require enormous psycho-emotional energy;

• Juggling creative activities (singing engagements) with teaching and dealing with a multitude of administrative and business issues; and

• Dealing with colleagues and students who are not supportive, due to disagreeable personality, opposing educational philosophy or teaching approach, or motivation that is competitive, non-cooperative, or hostile.

The Ultimate Reward of Teaching

These minor drawbacks aside, the teaching of singing can be an extremely fulfilling career choice. One well-known voice teacher, Patricia Misslin, a voice teacher now at the New England Conservatory in Boston, taught Renée Fleming, Stephanie Blythe and many others during a voice-teaching career spanning more than twenty years at the State University of New York in Potsdam. "There has never been a day in my life when I haven't learned something," Patricia Misslin told a writer for NOTES, a publication of the New England Conservatory. "That's what is fun about teaching: being stimulated all the time."

Notable Quotes: The Singer as Pedagogue

Why do some professional singers want to teach voice?

> At Westminster [Choir College, Rider University, Princeton, NJ], students started teaching in their first year, so that by the time they had gotten to their last year they knew whether or not they wanted to teach. I really look forward to the day when I can teach. I may be the only singer who feels that way in the whole world, because most of the people I know don't want to teach. I'm always talking to the younger singers, and they're always picking my brain. I'm not that old, but they know I'm out there doing it. I'm trying to compile from people in the know, people out there doing it, it could be a manual, it could be a lot of anecdotes, it could be checklists. I wish I'd had something like that. — Jennifer Larmore

> It's a very important feedback that you get from working with young people, because they're very straight. If you do things wrong, they will look at you and say, 'Tommy, you are wrong,' and so you are forced to think: 'Is my way correct or is it not?' My life has changed a lot in the six years that I have been teaching at Detmold. I'm much more balanced, much more relaxed, much more enthusiastic since I have been working with young people. — Thomas Quasthoff

Chapter 14

The Singer as Vocologist

What is Vocology?

One exciting trend in the voice profession is the emergence of a new type of voice expert known as a *vocologist*. This term refers to a comprehensively trained scientist-artist who explores and integrates data from all valid scientific and artistic resources. Ingo Titze, a renowned voice scientist and professor of voice at the University of Iowa, coined the term "vocology" to identify this new field encompassing interdisciplinary perspectives on voice. A vocologist can be trained either as a scientist (a speech pathologist, audiologist, or physicist), as a physician (otolaryngologist, neurologist, or endocrinologist), or as a singer, actor, voice teacher, or acting coach. A vocologist can thus function in the role of cross-trained scientist, physician, therapist, voice teacher, acting coach — or a combination of all of these.

One of Titze's doctoral students — an accomplished singer named Thea Engelson — humorously summed up the interdisciplinary nature of vocology in lyrics set to Gilbert and Sullivan's "I am the Very Model of a Modern Major

General", from *The Pirates of Penzance*:

I am the very model of a modern day vocologist
I represent a merger of a singer and a scientist
Biologist, musician, acoustician, also physicist!
With all this schizophrenia, I need a good psychiatrist.

(Titze, "A Modern-Day Vocologist", *Journal of Singing*, March/April, 1998).

Types of Vocologists

When a person experiences chronic laryngitis or other vocal pathology that inhibits normal vocal function, the first professional consulted is usually an *otolaryngologist*, a physician usually affiliated with an ENT (ear/nose/throat) clinic. After a thorough physical exam and interview, the physician may prescribe specific medication or treatment, including therapeutic rehabilitation under the guidance of a speech pathologist. Of course, not all physicians and speech pathologists are sufficiently experienced and trained to work with highly skilled voice professionals (singers, in particular), so care must be exercised in seeking only those highly recommended by reputable voice professionals.

Though legally prohibited from making a medical diagnosis, a well-qualified *speech pathologist* can identify standard vocal disorders during a laryngeal examination and interview. Typically, the speech pathologist will work with a patient for several weeks or longer in restoring and improving normal voice use.

If hearing problems occur, an *ENT physician* or *audiologist* is usually consulted. The physician examines a patient's auditory mechanism for physical abnormalities, while the audiologist conducts hearing tests and makes recommendations for measures to improve hearing, including the prescription of highly sensitive hearing aids.

The *voice scientist* is typically affiliated with an educational institution or a voice care clinic, and often serves in other roles such as researcher, teacher, journal editor, and writer. As is the case with the voice professionals discussed above, some noted voice scientists are also competent singers, such as Steve Austin, Thomas Cleveland, Scott McCoy, Ingo Titze, and Johan Sundberg. Voice scientists provide valuable research that explains various aspects of the vocal mechanism and how it functions.

And who are the artistic types of voice professionals? The major categories include singers, voice teachers, vocal coaches and theatrical voice coaches. In addition, several other types of voice professionals may give singers input and feedback, including conductors, stage directors and body movement specialists (Alexander Technique, Feldenkreis). Of course, the overall level of expertise varies considerably within each category; it is possible, for example, that some theatrical coaches or vocal coaches may actually be more skilled at identifying good singing than some singers or voice teachers.

Persons claiming to be vocologists demonstrate great interest in exploring the wide range of vocal information and expertise provided by all of the aforementioned voice professionals. Armed with such a comprehensive background of knowledge and skills, the vocologist enjoys considerable authority as a collaborative voice expert.

How We Came to Appreciate Vocology

Like most other young singers, I began my career by concentrating primarily on the singer's role. From my mid-20s to early 30s I was a singer-teacher, and in my late 30s to 40s I reversed those roles and became a teacher-singer. Finally, in my 50s I was mostly a pedagogue who gradually evolved into a vocologist.

Beginning in the 1970s, I became increasingly aware of the vocology movement. Voice publications, such as the NATS *Journal of Singing*, gradually increased the number and types of articles dedicated to such areas as vocal health, voice science, and pedagogy. There was also more attention given to creating interdisciplinary teams of voice experts in regional centers, with ongoing collaboration between such voice professionals as teachers, scientists, speech pathologists, and otolaryngologists.

At the University of Minnesota we have been fortunate to have several colleagues and a flow of graduate students who form a group known as the Vocology Consortium. Members of the group have included faculty, staff, and students from Communication Disorders, Otolaryngology, Music/Music Education, and Theater. Some of our efforts have included presenting colloquia on voice topics, undertaking joint research, and providing voice-team services in the local community. For example, I frequently ask Dr. Deirdre Michael, speech pathologist, to give lectures on acoustics and vocal health for my pedagogy classes and occasional workshops. I also engage Dr. George Goding, Jr, otolaryngologist, to give medical presentations. And, most importantly, when voice students or faculty experience problems, these experts willingly care for them. This interdisciplinary association has broadened my view of the voice profession and has enriched my teaching.

Ignorance of Vocology is Not Bliss

The emergence of vocology as a distinct field of study is very encouraging for the profession as a whole. But what can be done to remedy its apparent neglect in the professional voice community? Singers competent in other areas of vocal performance can be quite ignorant of vocal anatomy and physiology, acoustics, vocal dysfunction, and voice-related nomenclature.

For example, it is astounding to hear otherwise competent vocal performers use misleading anatomical statements, such as "I place my hands on my diaphragm, and sing from my stomach". Very revealing also is the fact that many singers mispronounce such common vocal terms as *larynx* (pronounced lai**rinks**, not lair**ninks**), and *pharynx* (fai**rinks**, not fair**ninks**) — even *accompanist* (accompa**nist**, not accompa**niest**). Bluntly put, it is incomprehensible why otherwise serious-minded singers would intentionally ignore the anatomical, physiological, and acoustical aspects of vocal production, and neglect to study the ways in which efficient singing serves creative vocal expression.

Singers are not alone in their neglect. Non-singing voice professionals may also exhibit a characteristic naïveté in certain areas of expertise. For instance, consider the typical speech pathologist who works frequently with distressed singers, but remains ignorant about the peculiar nature of the singing voice, especially classical singing technique. Furthermore, this type of speech pathologist may not fully understand efficient vocal production, and may be even less able to demonstrate it.

Despite these gaps, it is increasingly clear that voice professionals in the twenty-first century will be expected to possess comprehensive knowledge and training in vocology. Fortunately, great strides have been made in uniting the scientific and artistic voice communities, with mutual exchanges involving both traditional and cutting-edge knowledge and skills. In a growing spirit of collaboration, the artistic community of singers and voice teachers has joined with the scientific community of voice scientists, otolaryngologists, speech pathologists, and other voice professionals in public forums to share and disseminate relevant information. Such influential organizations as the National Association of Teachers of Singing and the Voice

Foundation have achieved a positive climate of cooperation and collaboration that bodes well for the future of vocal music education.

Though excellent progress has been made, many voice professionals still remain out of the "cross-fertilization" loop, with die-hards in both camps showing little respect for opposing viewpoints. For instance, a singer or voice teacher may resist accepting a certain voice scientist's research results, especially if the voice scientist is incapable of demonstrating adequate vocal technique. Conversely, a voice scientist may have little regard for a voice teacher who uses "singer's jargon" in place of standard scientific or medical terminology. Both sides have viewpoints worth exploring, so it's crucial that all parties listen to others, discussing differences with an open mind and seeking common ground.

Reciprocally, the scientific community needs to become familiar with the traditional knowledge and skills associated with singing. For example, non-singing voice professionals can gain valuable insight and experience by studying singing with competent voice teachers.

The Practical Core of Vocology

Anatomy and Biomechanics. A thorough understanding of basic vocal anatomy and biomechanics is essential to the vocologist. Aspects of biomechanics that come under the vocologist's scrutiny include respiratory function, muscle adduction/abduction, vocal-fold oscillation, control of loudness, pitch, register, and quality; physics of sound (acoustics); voice classification and voice changes across the lifespan. Traditional perceptual evaluation of singing output is used along with physical measures: glottography, videostroboscopy, electromyography, aerodynamic and acoustic analysis, and other measures.

Vocal Pathology. Here the vocologist considers normal deviations and fluctuations along with abnormal ones. For example, the vocologist studies culturally-based fluctuations, congenital disorders, neurological and muscular disorders, and tissue changes due to disease and aging. Some examples of disordered voice production include vocal abuse, vocal fatigue, and hoarseness. Some examples of common conditions and diseases needing treatment include laryngitis, spasmodic dysphonia, vocal fold motion impairment, polyps, vocal fold nodules and cysts, contact ulcers, and laryngeal cancer.

Vocal Rehabilitation. Here the vocologist is concerned with methods of intervention for the development, training, and rehabilitation of vocal behavior. These include motor learning and treatment strategies, techniques for relaxation, centered breath, efficient warm-up, resonance, articulation, register transitions, and muscle flexibility. They also may include assessment of therapeutic and teacher/student relationships.

A Unified Theory of Voice

The main idea of vocology is that the voice is a complete, unified instrument for human expression and communication. Singers may concentrate on improving their singing ability, while speech pathologists focus on assisting people with speech-related problems. In contrast, the vocologist is concerned with integrating polarities across the vocal spectrum. In other words, the human voice is approached as a single instrument that modulates freely between speech and singing, with a consistent vocal production that facilitates a wide range of expression.

In addition, the vocologist also recognizes at least five voice levels, beginning with conversational speech and moving through more energized levels (including elevated speech, dramatic speech), continuing to the level of recitative (or *Sprechgesang*), and finally to the ultimate level of vocalism: full-voiced singing. Most advanced-level voice practitioners communicate through these five levels of voice use, though the language and style of expression may vary considerably.

What are the characteristics of voice use at each level? The quietest level is *conversational speech,* an intimate form that varies from whispering to low dynamic levels, as illustrated by an intimate conversation between two lovers. The next step upward is *elevated speech,* as used by a speaker in a medium-sized room, for example, a teacher lecturing in a typical classroom. (We all know people who never speak below this level — for instance, the lone voice heard over a din of conversation in a busy restaurant, or the obnoxious cell phone user in a public place.) The third level is *dramatic speech,* as heard in Shakespearean drama, evangelistic preaching, or an oration by a fiery politician. So the three levels associated with speech are conversational, elevated, and dramatic, though dramatic speech approaches a quasi-singing hybrid stage that is very similar to recitative.

The fourth level — *recitative* or *Sprechgesang* — is familiar to vocal music aficionados as a hybrid form of speech-singing found in oratorio, opera, and musical theater. In the fifth and final level we have *full-voiced singing,* which is heard in several styles of vocal music, such as gospel, rock, oratorio, and opera. Generally speaking, "legitimate" full-voiced singing is heard primarily in classical vocal music, where the emphasis is placed on maximizing resonance — a technical maneuver that effectively involves throat, mouth, and nasal cavities of the entire vocal tract.

It should be stressed that ideal voice production should be consistent throughout the speaking and singing range, the only difference being the degree of energy used. The Italian admonition — "Cantare come si parla" (sing as you speak) — applies to all voice users, and it is equally true that one should speak as one sings. Of course, this dictum is based on efficient voice production in both speaking and singing. Inexplicably, most singers, including myself, tend to speak primarily using mouth resonance, partially explaining why mouth resonance predominates with untrained pop singers, as evidenced by tones that lack "ring" and *chiaroscuro* (bright/dark) characteristics.

All of the five voice levels can be discerned, analyzed, and executed effectively when one possesses a keenly developed ear. Paul Madaule claims that we control voice production essentially through bone conduction, with tone quality controlled by the right ear (the "musical ear"). Madaule's book, *When Listening Comes Alive: A Guide to Effective Learning and Communication* (Moulin Publishing, 1994), adds that since the ear is intricately involved in all mind-body activity, including movement and balance, sound stimulation is crucial to overcoming learning problems. Well-informed vocologists therefore pay special attention to the ear's role in speech and singing.

From Science to Art, and From Technique to Artistry

One of the ongoing controversies among voice professionals is how knowledge of vocal production specifically relates to performance. Voice experts with a scientific orientation tend to give more credence to objective, standardized research methods and techniques, with the intention of accurately identifying, describing, and documenting a wide range of vocal phenomena. On the other hand, although artists (performers) may use objective methods and techniques in voice development, repertoire study, and vocal performance, their overall tendency is to place greater emphasis on subjective matters, such as the effective interpretation and communication of vocal repertoire. The ideal singer is one who strikes a balance between technique and artistry.

Again, we raise the question: *What is technique, and why is it important in singing?* Essentially a left-brain activity, *technique* is concerned with the means, process, manner, or *how* a song is executed, according to specific mechanics and craft. Thus, a singer with good technique is one who knows how to produce efficient tone with ease, learn a song quickly and thoroughly, and communicate during performance using a wide range of vocal, musical, linguistic, and dramatic skills — comprehensive expertise that requires the long-term application of systematic methods and techniques.

Two additional steps are essential to developing artistry. First, singers must master the skill of *interpretation*, defined as the act of explaining or clarifying a song's essence (*what it's about*), according to the creative intentions of the composer, the textual source, and the performer (in that order). In conjunction with interpretation comes *expression*, the performance realization of a song in word, tone, and gesture that communicates something of the selection's essence to beholders. In other words, expression deals with *how* the intention of the composer and/or poet is interpreted or communicated.

Finally, we arrive at *artistry*, primarily a right-brain activity involved in forming a holistic, gestalt concept concerned with outcomes, including aesthetic qualities. Artistry serves as the ultimate answer, or the *why* response, to *what* is being expressed. Moreover, artistry is the desired outcome of creative imagination, a holistic process supported by technique, artistry's twin pillar in singing.

The well-rounded vocologist seeks to integrate all of the polarities that exist in the world of voice, particularly in science and art, speech and singing, and technique and artistry. Though expanding one's horizons to embrace the full spectrum of vocal knowledge and skill can be extremely challenging, the outcomes and rewards justify the effort. I hope this chapter inspires you to become a dedicated vocologist, the highest step on the evolutionary voice ladder.

Notable Quotes: The Singer as Vocologist

Who is a prominent singer who has suffered vocal problems that were cured with the help of voice and medical professionals?

> Encouragement by her fellow students kept Denyce Graves going through the Oberlin Conservatory in Ohio and the New England Conservatory in Boston. As she was getting into the audition and contest circuit, though, a throat ailment silenced her. Persistent pains in her vocal cords mystified doctors, and it looked as though her singing days were over. She took a job as a secretary. But along came a doctor who tracked her throat problems to a thyroid condition treatable by medication. After the Houston Grand Opera invited her to join its apprentice program, she moved to Texas and resumed her studying and singing in earnest. And in 1990, the Minnesota Opera hired her to do her first Carmen.
> — Steven Brown, Orlando Sentinel

How does knowledge of voice science help singers to understand voice quality, especially in terms of volume, timbre, and audibility?

> A singer like Pavarotti can be heard above an orchestra not because he's loud, but because he has a prominent

acoustical peak around 2900 hertz. If you filter that out, his voice disappears into the crowd. That prominent acoustical peak is the legendary fifth formant. It's called the "ring" or the "singer's formant," because typically, only professionally trained singers and actors can produce it. The untrained voice simply does not emit that frequency. — Robert Sataloff, MD

When somebody learns how to do the *ring*, they learn how to make part of the back of their throat very narrow, with a sudden expansion in the pharynx. It gives the most balanced sound in terms of high frequencies. — Ingo Titze

Chapter 15

The Singer as Colleague

Characteristics of a Good Colleague

Generally speaking, a *colleague* is an associate — in an office, a profession, or a type of work — with whom responsibility is shared, ideally within the framework of a supportive, constructive work environment. *Collegiality*, the act of being collegial (or a good colleague), is essential in promoting the highest standards of human achievement through the combined cooperative and collaborative efforts of many persons.

Healthy collegial relationships are built on four pillars: *ethics, communication, cooperation,* and *collaboration*. Thus, a good colleague:

- behaves humanely in all professional relationships, treating colleagues and associates with mutual respect and appreciation;

- communicates honestly, tactfully, and promptly with all colleagues and associates at appropriate times, particularly when working on projects of mutual interest;

- cooperates with colleagues and associates in supporting their professional and personal objectives; and
- collaborates enthusiastically and diligently on projects requiring shared participation.

These four characteristics illustrate healthy, positive behavior in working with colleagues as well as other associates, such as support staff. All of us are well aware of unpleasant work situations involving colleagues who refuse to communicate or cooperate with one another. Usually, such occurrences are the result of minor offenses and misunderstandings that have remained unresolved over time. Who hasn't heard such comments as: "Since he didn't attend my recital, I'll make it a point not to attend his upcoming performance"; or, "She didn't have one positive comment to offer regarding my performance, so she must not like what I did." As we've all learned, unfounded assumptions about people's intentions or actions often lead to overblown, overreactive behavior.

One common problem on the job is the presence of unfounded gossip and hearsay spread by bitter or envious co-workers. Bad-mouthing colleagues, for whatever reason, is an all-too-common occurrence in the music profession. Stories of hostile rivalries involving certain singers, voice teachers, conductors, stage directors, and others within the vocal profession are common knowledge. Admittedly, it's not easy to hold one's tongue in the spreading of gossip or in venting ill feelings, especially if one has been treated badly. The psycho-emotional effort it takes to "walk in the other person's shoes", or to attempt reconciliation through one-on-one dialogue requires considerable good will and open communication. On the other hand, ill will is a potentially destructive force, spreading outward concentrically and affecting everyone within contact of the warring parties.

In sum, a good colleague makes every effort to avoid creating unhealthy relationships, and when problems arise, seeks prompt, lasting solutions. Moreover, a supportive colleague makes every effort to cooperate and collaborate effectively with fellow colleagues.

The Vocal Colleague as Gatekeeper

In the vocal music profession the gatekeeper is the standard-bearer. No matter what area or type of vocal music genre, be it popular music or classical, high levels of professional expectations need to be promoted, safeguarded, and upheld. The model singer, voice teacher, coach, conductor, director, and other voice professionals serve as gatekeepers, allowing only the most talented, promising, and accomplished persons to enter their particular professional discipline.

For instance, college and university-level voice instructors hear numerous students annually in entrance auditions for undergraduate and graduate voice programs. At all levels, from beginning (freshmen) and intermediate (juniors through first-year masters) to advanced (doctoral level), fairly uniform standards for admitting qualified students to music programs are established throughout the higher education system. Most voice professionals concur that admitting unqualified students may be considered a form of professional dishonesty, particularly when competition for gainful employment within the vocal profession is extremely intense, and remuneration is modest.

For similar reasons, entrance standards in professional singing fields are set even higher. For instance, musical organizations affiliated with the American Guild of Musical Artists (AGMA) agree to certain contractual terms and working conditions for vocal music artists, with stringent guidelines and practices for hiring singers strongly enforced. The reality is that agents, conductors, and others responsible for auditioning and hiring singers are expected to maintain the highest professional standards. As happens in all professions, however, there is no guarantee that everyone admitted into the profession will survive. We've all heard tales of singers who started out as flaming stars, but for various reasons crashed and burned, eventually finding themselves unemployed in their chosen profession.

The Vocal Colleague as Mentor

A *mentor* is usually thought of as a wise, experienced, trusted friend and advisor. When a mature singer or artist-teacher takes under his or her wing a budding young singer and guides the newcomer toward a professional career, he or she may be termed a "mentor". Such a relationship normally begins as a traditional student-teacher relationship, when the young singer is learning the basics of the vocal profession. By the time a budding singer is sufficiently skilled to begin singing at more advanced levels, as typically occurs at the graduate level in the mid- to-late 20s, more professional opportunities may surface, including professional singing engagements or part-time teaching positions. The student's teacher may gradually take the role more as colleague than mentor, particularly upon graduation when a search for full-time employment commences. This relationship may continue for years, as the mentor guides the younger singer or teacher through the first part of his or her professional career. Over time, the relationship becomes more and more collegial, as the younger person achieves a higher status in the profession.

Though singers may serve as mentors at various levels and ages, mentoring usually requires a certain loss of ego that can only be acquired through age and experience. For this reason, most singers become effective mentors only when solidly in the prime of their careers, feeling unthreatened and secure with their level of achievement. As respectable models, they are able to impart much wisdom and practical advice about the many pitfalls and challenges young singers face in the professional world. Likewise, in academia most effective mentors are those who have achieved a certain level of success, including tenure at the associate professor level. In many cases, these artists-teachers have performed widely, perhaps even professionally for several years, and have also adjusted to the rigors of teaching in academia. The knowledge such mentors can pass along to their protégées can be invaluable in helping them cope as young professionals.

I strongly advise singers to seek a mentor-type teacher who fulfills the above description. At the outset of your vocal career, it is to your ultimate advantage to cultivate a long-term collaborative relationship with any prospective mentor.

The services of a supportive mentor are enhanced by your demonstration of responsible personal behavior and serious motivational commitment as a singer, and by your show of sincere respect and appreciation for the mentor both on professional and personal levels. It never hurts to prove your good will by volunteering to help him or her in some constructive way, for instance by assisting with class or studio management or helping with refreshments for an official occasion (recitals, student parties). The idea is to develop a reciprocal relationship involving giving and receiving by both parties.

A word about giving and receiving gifts is in order. Every teacher/mentor has an opinion on gift-giving, and I suspect age has something to do with it. Though I'm not opposed to receiving gifts on special occasions from students, I certainly don't expect or solicit them. It seems the older one gets, the less need or desire there is to accumulate items that add to clutter at home or in the studio. Instead, I particularly appreciate a student inviting me out for an inexpensive meal, sending a card of appreciation that contains a heartfelt message, or, if a gift is necessary, presenting special items I can use. Finding an appropriate gift may require some research, but it seems worth the effort.

And what about teachers presenting gifts to students? Teachers vary in their attitudes about gift giving, but I believe they should rarely be given, and then only in recognition of very special achievements or occasions such as weddings or graduations. Though teachers must be careful to not show partiality to certain students, there will always be some students with whom they are closer, perhaps due to a long-time association. In any case, the greatest gift a teacher can give a student is selfless, devoted attention and skillful expertise.

When separated from your mentor, as during summer vacations, try to maintain personal contact by means of an occasional email, postcard, or phone call reporting your activities and inquiring about your mentor's activities. Even a general newsletter sent to certain interested persons will suffice.

If you demonstrate your loyalty and respect through positive actions, your mentor will be more willing to reciprocate in supporting your goals and objectives. The same advice applies to mentors, most of whom are eager to maintain contact with the students they have invested considerable time and effort in helping.

The Vocal Colleague as Lifecycle Exemplar

Singers wear different hats at different stages of life. For example, an older singer may excel as a mentor, but a young singer may not be expected to perform in such a role. On the other hand, a young singer may be more adept at performance than an older singer who has retired from an active performance career.

Again, referencing Joseph Campbell's book, *Reflections on the Art of Living*, we look at the major stages of human life (adapted to make relevant connections to singers' roles).

- *Childhood/Youth* **(to 20s).** The student role requires obedience and conformity to the patterns and rules of society; and singers learn the basic information, skills, and rules applicable in building a vocal music career.

- *Young Adulthood* **(to 40s).** The responsible "Thou Shalt" adult life stage, is marked by adherence to laws of social order; choosing and assuming responsibilities, and achieving position and fame in the world. Singers at this stage are normally in their performance prime and are well established in their careers, with their youth and vitality intact.

- *Midlife Adulthood* **(to 50s).** For a vocal musician, the self-discovery and "follow your bliss" realization stage holds diminishing expectations of rewards for being good or punishments for being bad. Inappropriate ego issues are released as one becomes more concerned with matters of the heart, for example, giving more attention to family and friends than to achievement or prestige. Singers, growing older and encountering possible age discrimination, may decide to step down from active performing careers to pursue other options, such as teaching voice and mentoring students.

- *Senior Adulthood* **(to 70s).** The self-reassessment and new beginnings stage is marked by retirement from full-time work and possibly the pursuit of interesting part-time employment such as teaching and mentoring students. This is a time to prepare for old age with meaningful activities such as travel, hobbies, and increasing attention to family and friends.

- *Old Age* **(beyond 80s).** This is the survival mode and stage, the purpose of which includes reflections on life, dying, and death, and, ideally, transcendence that transports one beyond the confines of the physical world.

Who are model singers for graceful aging? Of numerous models of aging singers who continue to use their voices efficiently and expressively, two deserve special mention. In October of 2002, Oren Brown, an active, internationally known 93-year-old teacher-singer, gave exhilarating presentations at a conference entitled *The Aging Singer: The Reality and the Hope*. He also performed admirably in a Senior Showcase, the culmination of the day's events. One could hope to be as mentally and physically active as Dr. Brown, if we are fortunate to reach such a ripe age.

Another role model is Agnes Lisowsky, who at the age of 97 was reported to have 16 students taking voice lessons each week in her home. She claims, "I can't sit around and do nothing. All I've done all my life is teach music. Without this work, I'd fade away." To hear and diagnose student vocalism seems a major achievement at such an age, but to teach them well is remarkable indeed.

The ideal vocal colleague is one who feels a strong sense of responsibility not only to contemporaries but also to those aspiring to enter the profession. My hope is that all singers will strive to become exemplary role models, thereby raising the standards of singing and enhancing human communication through expressive performances.

Notable Quotes: The Singer as Colleague

What positive personal characteristics do the greatest singers demonstrate?

> Plácido Domingo will cross a continent or an ocean to help a friend or a cause. In 1985 he canceled dozens of performances to raise money for Mexican earthquake relief. In 1988 he flew from New York to the Seattle bedside of onetime rival Jose Carreras, who was near death from leukemia. When tenor Carlo Cossutta was indisposed at the last minute for the gala season opener of the San Francisco Opera in 1983, Domingo jumped out of New York rehearsals and into a Learjet in New York on a few minutes' notice and streaked west as an emergency Otello. He donned his makeup and costume on the plane. — Ken Ringle, *The Washington Post*

> Something I've noticed about the greatest singers is their generosity. Marilyn Horne's been a mentor to me for the last two years — I call her every time I have a problem to ask what should I do about? Joan Sutherland — I went to her house one day and she told me how to sing high notes. Caballé talked about the fact that she made the best part of her career in the bel canto repertoire but she said, "You know, I never really had the top." Just give me Leontyne Price's high notes, Caballé's pianissimo. — Renée Fleming

How does an aging singer adjust to changes in the voice?

> Someday I will disappear. But I hope to sing until then. I need this Fountain of Youth, the Fountain of Love, this expansion of myself through my voice. It is a part of my private life as much as my sons, my

family. I need it like food for my soul. I have done one thing in the fifty years of my career — I have always put a lot of love out to people. So you have planted the seeds, and finally you have the *recompesa* — people love you not only as a singer. It becomes that you are loved as a person. It has nothing to do with if you sing better or not better, if you are not as you were before. The people love me with wrinkles now — yes, it's true! And I think much better than before. I am now as I was when I was twenty-five years old. I was nobody, and I am still nobody. I am a human being like others, you see, and people feel this. They feel, 'Victoria is like us, except she sings.' That, I think, is most important. This is life, true life. The other things are all vanity. — Victoria De Los Angeles

As we get older, we all go through processes of having to reexamine and reinvent ourselves. Over the last three or four years my voice has changed a bit. It's gotten a little darker and there are roles that don't really fit me as well as they did ten or twelve years ago. But, there are roles that now at my age I can sing that I didn't ever think that I could before. Everybody has to go through a period of reassessing and asking themselves, 'where am I vocally, where am I psychologically, where am I spiritually and where am I emotionally?' — Jerry Hadley

Part IV
Serving Self and Others

Chapter 16

The Singer as Collaborator

Interpersonal Relationships

A singer rarely performs alone, completely isolated from others, except in the privacy of a practice space. Most vocal performances require a close collaboration between two or more artists, beginning with the duo team of singer and accompanist and extending to large ensembles, such as opera, which require many levels of interpersonal relationships.

Talented singers can be seriously hindered in the pursuit of their career objectives if they have difficulty working well with others. A very effective communication grapevine exists in the singing world, particularly in opera circles, so artists of a temperamental and uncooperative nature are usually placed on an informal "undesirable colleague" list. In other words, they are labeled as persons to be avoided, and ultimately, not to be hired.

The majority of interpersonal conflicts can be traced to negative personal traits, including the following:

• *Negative attitudes*. A negative attitude that results in excessive criticism or unfounded gossip, either overt or covert, is perhaps the most common behavior problem. Throughout my career I've encountered many persons with bad attitudes. I try to abide by the proverb, "We reap what we sow", as well as "What goes around, comes around". Thus, purveyors of ill will tend to get back exactly what they dish out, usually in the form of silent banishment from the world of singing.

- *Habitual tardiness or absence.* When singers are late for rehearsals, or miss them altogether, disrespect for colleagues is inadvertently communicated. While it is not disastrous for a single chorister to miss a rehearsal or performance, when a solo singer misses, the consequences can become serious, especially in small ensembles. I recall several situations when rehearsals had to be rearranged or rescheduled because key singers failed to show up, and the resulting working atmosphere was unpleasant. Though there may be valid reasons for tardiness or absenteeism, forgetfulness or carelessness are usually resented.

- *Differences in perceptual modes and styles.* People with different learning modes and styles may develop misunderstandings because of their inability to empathize with one another's perceptions and behaviors. For example, an analytical or visual-mode singer may not be able to fathom why an aural-mode singer can't sight-sing music more quickly. Likewise, the aural singer may not grasp why an analytical or visual singer can't sing with a more beautiful, expressive tone quality.

- *Philosophical differences.* Depending on what aspect of singing is being discussed, philosophical positions can vary immensely. If the topic is ethics, then we're dealing with moral behavior; whereas if aesthetics is the subject, the emphasis may focus on the type, quality, and presentation of vocal repertoire. For example, a singer's preference for certain types of vocal music will determine stylistic and vocal presentations, as demonstrated by the conflicts between aficionados of classical and non-classical idioms. Though I'm not a fan of rap music, I appreciate the vitality of the rhythm, inventive lyrics, and soulful delivery presented by rap singers. Moreover, there are some classical vocal works I'd just as soon avoid, especially the atonal, noisy, unvocal, difficult variety.

• *Physical mannerisms and personal hygiene issues.* For some people certain mannerisms may be offensive, and for good reason. We can all think of uncouth mannerisms that offend: nose picking, belching, ear cleaning, and certain obscene gestures. Moreover, who wants to be in close proximity to a singer with foul breath, grimy clothes, greasy hair, or offensive body odor? Or what about the dolled-up singer sporting strong perfume, hairspray, or other allergenic chemicals? (Whew! It's time for some fresh air.)

• *Incompatible music-making opinions.* Many conflicts among singers and instrumentalists arise over technical, musical, stylistic, linguistic, interpretive and presentational considerations. Disagreements may reach fever heights, with one or more performers insisting on a single way to perform a composition. There is usually no "perfect" way to perform a given composition, for each performance should be unique, determined by the collective intelligence and artistry of the performers involved. One of my pet peeves is conductors who insist that their interpretation, including tempi, dynamics, and style, is the only true way to perform certain works. Such autocratic conducting style tends to stifle the performers as it creates stiff, stressful performing conditions. I've been fortunate over the years to have worked on several premiere or near-premiere performances with live American composers including Dominick Argento, Aaron Copland, Gordon Binkerd,

Charles Sjogren, David E. Thomas, and David King. To my pleasant surprise, each of these composers was very flexible and willing to make adjustments to suit the performers' capabilities. Such experiences lead me to surmise that the great composers we revere from the past would also have been willing to make adjustments in their works to accommodate performers, as long as the overall performance was effective.

Competition versus Collaboration

Humans use two basic models of social intercourse, one competitive and the other collaborative, both of which are applicable to vocal performance.

- The *competitive* model encourages a spirit of individualism that motivates one to maximize personal gain, sometimes without concern for the gains or losses of others. In competitive situations, singers vie to outdo one another.

- The *collaborative* model encourages a shared sense of community and purpose. By fostering interpersonal relationships and understanding, a collaborative ethic engenders a positive learning and work environment as individuals band together to work on shared goals.

Though competitive and collaborative models may appear diametrically opposed, both can be used to create favorable learning and working conditions. For example, while singing demands considerable individual effort to improve overall performance level (competition model), it is equally important that singers have an appropriate social context in which they can experiment (collaborative model). Practically all activities common to career singers or artist-teachers provide competitive and collaborative opportunities, beginning with educational training (classes, ensembles) and continuing throughout a singer's professional life.

How do "cooperative" and "collaborative" working models differ? Individuals who cooperate often reach some agreement but proceed individually toward self-determined goals, while people who collaborate work closely together and share mutual responsibility for their joint endeavor. In addition to involving cooperative action, collaboration emerges from shared goals and leads to outcomes that benefit all partners. Thus, an example of cooperation may be mutual agreements between a singer and other musicians regarding rehearsal scheduling and type of repertoire to be learned for a certain performance, while collaboration may be exemplified by the mutual action undertaken by all in rehearsing and performing the agreed-upon repertoire.

According to Daniel Goleman, author of *Emotional Intelligence* (1995), we are guided in all interpersonal relationships by our "emotional intelligence," which is seen through such empathetic traits as self-restraint and compassion — the ability to "tune-in" to others' feelings and actions. Strong interpersonal relationships depend upon open lines of communication and a sense of equality or "fair play."

Strengthening Collaborative Relationships

Among the significant collaborations a singer experiences is working one-on-one with colleagues such as a voice teacher, accompanist, accompanist-coach, conductor, or stage director. In such intimate collaborations, it helps if individuals view the relationship as a partnership, with each person held in mutual high esteem and respect, and each person offering input that affects all decisions. Differences that arise are discussed calmly and rationally, the objective being to reach an appropriate compromise or middle ground. For example, if an accompanist-coach questions any aspect of a singer's rendition (tempi, style, diction, interpretation, etc.), the singer is willing and able to offer reasonable explanations. The same rule applies to the accompanist-coach.

In groups of three or more persons, interpersonal dynamics are heightened, and there is need for greater self-control. Since individual emotional flare-ups in groups can be demoralizing and detrimental to the collective effort, singers should study techniques for restraining and calming strong emotions. Those who hire singers look for team players who can submerge their strong individualistic artistic temperaments for the good of the entire ensemble.

When collaborative differences are the result of personality conflicts or incompatible artistic opinions, singers should remain level headed and open-minded. From the singer's perspective, it is not collaborative when, during an orchestral rehearsal for a pending performance, a conductor attempts to pacify a singer's concern about specific tempi in a difficult aria by saying, "Don't worry, I'll just follow you." Inevitably, this type of conductor will indeed *follow* the singer, lagging behind at least a beat or so most of the way (as I've experienced on several occasions).

So how does one handle such a situation? The singer may tactfully suggest a private session at the conclusion of the orchestral rehearsal or at a more convenient time. Furthermore, a singer should not automatically submit to a stage director's command to perform a demanding physical activity that might hinder optimal vocalism and detract from the drama. Yet, in a collaborative spirit, the singer is advised to make an attempt to execute requested maneuvers before voicing any private objections, which are best scheduled at convenient times following rehearsals. Although people usually feel threatened when having their authority questioned in the presence of others, they tend to relate with more equanimity in one-on-one confrontations.

Leadership guru Stephen R. Covey, author of *The Seven Habits of Highly Effective People* (1989), offers principles to increase our effectiveness in relating to others. Here is a brief summary:

- *Be proactive.* The habit of personal vision requires taking responsibility (*response/ability*) for one's thoughts and actions.

- *Begin with the end in mind.* The habit of personal leadership requires beginning each new day with a clear understanding of one's desired goals and objectives.

- *Put first things first.* The habit of personal management requires organizing and managing time and events around the personal priorities identified in habit number two.

- *Think win/win.* The habit of interpersonal leadership requires the cooperative and collaborative efforts of two or more persons.

- *Seek first to understand, then to be understood.* The habit of empathic communication requires the art of listening and being attentive to others' desires and needs.

- *Synergize.* The habit of creative cooperation or teamwork creates a synergy that results from integrating diverse perspectives and differences.

- *Sharpen the saw.* The habit of self-renewal requires having a systematic program in four areas of living: physical, mental, emotional/social, and spiritual.

Talented, skillful singers who develop these seven time-tested personal habits will be rewarded in their professional careers and personal lives, with the likelihood of increased performance opportunities and greater happiness in their social relationships.

Notable Quotes: The Singer as Collaborator

How do professional singers feel about collaborating with colleagues on music projects?

> You have to be able to collaborate – you have to be able to work. If a director asks you to do something and your first response is "no," then neither he nor you can get a good product. But if a director asks me to do something that is not absolutely ridiculous, like hanging upside down with your head in a bucket of water, then I will try it. — Jennifer Larmore

> Collaboration has always been important to me and finding collaborators I felt at home with, people I could be myself with, has been very important to me . . . Jimmy Levine [Conductor James Levine] has been a very important collaborator and mentor. This relationship has led me in a very different direction. My appreciation for Jan de Gaetani, my love for the kind of music-making that she did and the way that she spoke about music with me led me to think about music differently and to see my own place in the world of performing differently, that kind of led me down another path. — Dawn Upshaw

> In all my recital contracts, it is stated that the accompanist must be mentioned in all the publicity. We're a team, and I don't think it can work if you're not. — Jennifer Larmore

Chapter 17
The Singer as Healer

Mozart and the "Vocal Effect"

Don Campbell's best selling book, *The Mozart Effect* (1997), explores the profound influence that sound (music) has on mind-body growth, development, and healing. Singers should study this "vocal effect" to learn more about the psychophysical (mind-body) effects of sound vibrations on both singers and listeners.

Interestingly, the word "sound" stems from the Middle English word *gesund,* akin to the German word for healthy. The English word *health* comes from Middle English *helthe,* derived from *hal,* which means *whole.* Common expressions associated with mind-body health include "in tune", "in harmony", "sympathetic chord", and "same wave length." Even the word "person" (*per-son*) is derived from the meaning "sound passes through."

Sound may be thought of as a form of energy that can be organized in various ways — shapes, patterns, figures, and mathematical proportions — and can be manifested through environmental noise, music, speech, and other vocal utterances. Both regular and irregular vibrations (sound-waves) assault our minds and bodies constantly, including the barrage of vocal sounds we utter in communicating our innermost thoughts and feelings. Sound is measured in frequencies (16-20,000 hertz is detectable by the human ear), intensities (pain is experienced at 125 decibels), and timbre (the quality of tone as determined by overtones).

Alfred Tomatis, MD, an expert in sonic detection, believes that high frequencies (3000-8000 hertz) are felt in the brain and affect cognitive functions. Medium frequencies (750-3000 hertz) stimulate the heart, lungs, and emotions, and low frequencies (125-750 hertz) affect physical movement, as when a low-pitched drone causes grogginess. From common experience and scientific studies we know that loud, irregular noise can be debilitating, while gentle, low-paced music is soothing and uplifting.

So what type of music ranks highest in assisting mind-body health? Scientific studies show that, in general, classical music provides more benefits. Not surprisingly, Mozart's music ranks highest, presumably because it is well balanced, elegant, direct, serene, inventive, and deeply felt. According to studies at the University of California-Irvine, Mozart's music also improves learning and concentration, as demonstrated by the improved test scores of students who listen to Mozart before and during testing. In fact, singers are often measured by how well they are able to perform Mozart's vocal music, chiefly because it requires a dependable vocal technique based on tonal beauty, flexibility, sustaining power, and a consistency of bright/dark timbre throughout one's vocal range.

The Healing Role of Breath-Tone in Mind-Body Health

In all types of vocal activity, especially singing, energy is channeled and released largely through breath, known in Asian religions as *prana* or *ki*, the life force on which vocal sound is transported. From the primal birth cry to vocal utterances, speech, singing, and the final gasp of death, we are inextricably bound to breathing and sound making. According to Don Campbell, a singer's built-in sound system — breath, ears, voice, and choice of music or self-generated sounds — is the most powerful known medium for healing. All forms of vocalization can be therapeutic, but *toning*, the sustaining of a predetermined optimal pitch, can be especially beneficial by way of oxygenating the body, deepening breathing, relaxing muscles, and stimulating energy flow. In short, a rich-toned timbre will help massage and tune up the entire body, with positive results on immune function.

Naturally, we're concerned with how we can use singing for healing ourselves and others. The principal objective of vocal healing is to maximize sound vibrations throughout the body, beginning with well-balanced, coordinated vocal production that sets up the following conditions:

- a calm, well-focused psycho-emotional state (yoga breath exercises);

- a proper alignment of the body and the vocal tract (a gentle upward stretch, achieved by lifting the head at the crown);

- a release of unnecessary muscle tension, especially in the breathing system and articulators (jaw, tongue, lips, etc.);

- a relaxed, deep, and expansive breath achieved by maintaining the gesture-of-inhalation during singing; and

- an image of energetically releasing breath-tone in a high-arched up-and-over pattern when vocalizing (see page 92).

By using a vigorous hum based on an "m" or an "ng", maximum vibrations may be experienced. The more coordinated the vocal output, the more vibrations are sensed. A full range of overtones creates sympathetic vibrations in regions of the head, throat-mouth, and chest, depending in large part on the frequency (pitch) and intensity (decibel) of the tone. An unrestricted, well-functioning voice will produce more vibrations than a hyper-functional, restricted vocal production. So, when the vocalized tone is efficiently produced, head and body vibrations are maximized, and so, too, are the health effects on singer and audience.

And what about high notes? There's probably a "sound reason" for the positive reaction people have when listening to or producing fully resonated, powerful high notes. Most singers report an incomparable exhilaration when vocalizing high notes, and everyone is emotionally transported when hearing an accomplished tenor, such as Pavarotti, singing the climax of the aria, "Nessun dorma," as it majestically soars up to the final word, "vincero." Perhaps, in addition to the psycho-emotional associations and story line of the opera *Turandot*, we are simply responding to the sound itself, with its multiple overtones, high intensity level, and overall tonal characteristics.

Individual Cases

I have long appreciated the positive effects of singing on overall health, based on observation of many singers I have taught or known. Following are some brief stories that illustrate the power of singing on mind-body health.

I recall a graduate soprano who studied with me in the 70s, at a time when I unfortunately had neither a firm grasp on vocal technique, nor a holistic view of singing. Susan (not her real name) was in her mid 30s, married, and miserable in her personal and professional life. The small town she lived in provided few vocal outlets, and her husband, who was not a musician, was unsupportive. She felt isolated from the vocal mainstream, and was only truly happy when singing away from her hometown. Though singing made her feel whole, her inability to expand her singing career was extremely demoralizing. She was often teary eyed in lessons, yet when she performed she looked radiant and happy. Singing kept her going, and healed her isolation.

Another student reported that breathing exercises and vocal routines used in voice class (and practiced daily) had given her noticeable relief from continuous back pain from a car accident several years earlier. She reported that the breathing, stretching, and vocal exercises performed in voice class provided the best medicine she'd ever received for the back pain stemming from her injuries. Other students have reported health improvements through singing. Indeed, the noble profession of music therapy is dedicated to helping people heal through music.

Mind-Body Strategies

Early in my career I experienced muscle tensions in my torso and head-neck area which contributed to developing a faulty vocal technique. My voice was frequently tired after singing for longer periods, with labored phonation, and occasionally with temporary hoarseness. It was very frustrating, as I had highly visible engagements to fulfill, and sometimes feared I might not make it through a long recital or opera role. This experience motivated me to study the workings of the voice, and resulted in developing a healthy vocal technique for my senior years.

This personal history brings to mind Matthias Alexander, the nineteenth-century Australian actor who was vocally debilitated due to faulty vocal technique presumably caused by excessive body tensions. After laborious self-study,

Alexander developed his well-known mind-body strategy, the Alexander Technique, which focuses on harmonious body alignment and movement, consequently enabling a more flexible and responsive vocal mechanism (Heirich, 1993). In like manner, Moshe Feldenkreis, in seeking a method to avoid wheelchair confinement after a serious knee injury, developed a self-discovery process based on movement and learning to perform with minimum effort and maximum efficiency (Blades-Zeller 2002).

Singing is liberating to the body, mind, and spirit. When singing I often feel that I'm getting a physical workout, and my voice feels fresh. The extra vibrations, especially in the head, are rejuvenating. The breath energy required gets my whole metabolism pumping, and I enjoy the workout.

In sum, it seems appropriate to paraphrase the familiar directive, "Physician, heal thyself," by modifying and expanding it to: "Singer, heal thyself, and others as well." Based on what we've learned, maximizing sound vibrations in daily voice use will not only increase communication skills, but also enhance mind-body wellness.

Notable Quotes: The Singer as Healer

What physical and emotional challenges do singers face?

> Once during a *Gioconda* [by Ponchielli] at the Metropolitan in New York I had to leave during a performance because of a cold, panic-stricken, with the sudden feeling of being terribly human, fallible, ordinary, like anyone else. Except that a person who suffers from a cold does not go to the office. An artist has to give his best. The voice collects and translates your bad physical health, your emotional worries, your personal troubles. If a problem

is undermining you, the smallest performance becomes an insuperable obstacle. You dread it. Then, miraculously, you clear the hurdle. Because, to assume your part on that day, you had to relativize your problem, erase it progressively from your mind and then brush it aside. Singing becomes a form of therapy. — Plácido Domingo

Thomas Quasthoff, 40, stands just four feet tall on legs that were stunted at birth, the consequence of a thalidomide pregnancy. He has almost no arms, his hands emerging just below the shoulders . . . In 1988, aged 28, he won a national competition in Munich and was hailed by Fischer-Dieskau, no less, for his "wondrously beautiful voice". "I have a problem when people say I should be a hero for others who are disabled, because I don't live a disabled life. I have a beautiful, tall girlfriend and I live a normal life. . . When I am singing, I feel completely happy. It's my world. I get to express myself with my own voice; to touch people with it is the most beautiful thing."
— Norman Lebrecht

What healing role does a singer fulfill, both personally and for others?

Denyce Graves' 2001-2002 season began with a series of appearances in response to the tragic events in New York City, Washington, D.C., and Shanksville, Pennsylvania on September 11, 2001. Ms. Graves was invited by President Bush to participate in the National Prayer Service in Washington's National Cathedral in which she sang "America, the Beautiful", and "The Lord's Prayer". This event was televised worldwide and was followed by Ms. Graves' appearance on The Oprah Winfrey Show in a live musical program of 'Healing through Gospel Music.' Ms. Graves has since participated in other benefit concerts, and RCA Records released a recording of patriotic songs by Ms. Graves, the proceeds of which have gone to groups affected by the events of September 11. — online biography

I was asked to sing "Amazing Grace" at Ground Zero. I couldn't look at the faces, once I began. It wasn't until sometime later that I had the realization about why I was there: to bring music, to comfort and provide solace for these [hurting] people. — Renée Fleming, addressing 2003 graduates of the Juilliard School, New York City

Chapter 18

The Singer as Caregiver

The Typical Singer's Stressful Lifestyle

It's common knowledge that the career track of the highly competitive singer affords limited opportunity for achieving artistic — or financial — success. In spite of such disheartening prospects, ambitious young singers are often determined to "make it", regardless of the potential pitfalls, which include a stressful lifestyle.

Stress levels spike immediately during the freshman year of college, when music students begin to undertake an intensive curriculum that includes demanding courses such as music theory, ear-training, and performance ensembles, each of which requires more time and effort than the credit-level usually reflects. Freshmen and sophomore music majors experience a more demanding schedule than students in other majors, primarily because music is one of the few disciplines that begin in the freshman year (most majors begin in the junior year). Consequently, the overall dropout rate of freshmen music students is quite high, especially for vocal performance majors who lack strong skills in theory, keyboard, and sight-singing.

Elsewhere I have mentioned my personal struggles with music theory courses, as well as evolving career plans, throughout my undergraduate years. Add to the complexity the fact that my wife and I sealed our marriage vows when I was a junior and she was a sophomore. Also, before graduating we became parents, adding to the collective responsibilities of school, part-time employment, performance engagements, and a limited social life. By the time we were in our mid 20s, we had three young sons, so you can imagine how busy we were trying to juggle a multitude of responsibilities. Fortunately, we managed to survive our first few years of married life relatively well, thanks in large part to parental support and a modest lifestyle. Today, young adults are faced with some of the same challenges, plus some other stressors that make life even more complicated. And this brings us to what typically happens when singers complete their formal education.

When a career-bound singer is in the final stages of vocal music training, whether it is in graduate school, an apprentice program, or working as a semi-professional performer, additional pressures begin to build. As the crucial "make or break" cut-off age approaches (around age 30), anxiety naturally increases. Non-music interests, including personal relationships (spouse, partner, children, parents), lifestyle (finances, home environment) and social life inevitably move to center stage, providing increasing competition with career objectives. For some students, doors may open when they receive invitations or positive feedback from gatekeepers, mentors, and respected colleagues. For other students, a crisis may erupt if they fail to gain steady professional performing opportunities.

Classical Singer, an indispensable professional-oriented magazine for singers, published an entire issue (March 1999) devoted to psychological topics associated with the numerous lifestyle challenges encountered by the typical career-bound singer. The general theme, "Depression and Singers", was explored through articles about situations singers experience at crucial points in their careers, including managing loneliness on the road, maintaining personal relationships with partners, children, and friends, coping with rejection, and dealing with financial uncertainty caused by sporadic, underpaid employment.

While some young singers enjoy well-rounded, balanced lifestyles, the typical upwardly mobile singer's life is frequently out of control, with work and career determining every aspect of life. Even when recreating or socializing, topics related to singing tend to pre-occupy or at least slip into most singers' conversations. To counteract an obsession with work, a healthy singer needs to explore, develop, and maintain other aspects of his or her personality, especially non-music talents and interests. Periodic breaks from music and singing are essential to a balanced lifestyle.

How Singers Do It

How can singers counteract the destructive aspects of their chosen profession? As the popular aphorism goes, "Get a Life!" In a *20/20* TV news program interview (January 2000), the noted soprano Renée Fleming stated her number one goal is to live a good life, implying that her singing career is a secondary consideration. Likewise, the well-known conductor Stephen Lord affirms that the true life of music is not simply the life of performing, which is secondary to a singer's contribution to the betterment of the people listening (*Opera News,* September 2003).

The secret for aspiring artists seems to be to create a life that encompasses the role of singer, yet transcends singing in the overall picture. The older I become, the more I believe it is important to seek and develop interests outside singing. For me, it might mean returning to the artwork I enjoyed so much as a child, before the singing bug bit me. I also turned more to writing, which I discovered later in my career. Though I'd written academic papers as an undergraduate and graduate student, I never considered myself a writer. After I began writing about singing, it gradually occurred to me that I enjoyed it.

At a young age we really can't know what paths our life will take, or what new endeavors will develop into fervent avocations. All we can do at the outset is be open to possibilities, all the while preparing ourself thoroughly to take advantage of opportunities as they come along.

The Importance of Family and Close Friends

One of the ways to stay balanced and grounded is give care to others. The term "care-giver" refers to the concern, attention, and care a singer gives to important persons in his or her life: parents, spouse or partner, children, grandparents, uncles, aunts, cousins, close friends, and so on. As we said before, the typical professional singer's lifestyle can be very stressful, requiring irregular work hours, late nights, and considerable travel. Many personal relationships are strained to the breaking point due to the singer's inability to cope effectively with the inherent stresses of a vocal music career.

In the end, each singer must decide what type of lifestyle he or she wants to live, and then determine the measures needed to achieve it. Setting lifestyle priorities is a first step. If a professional singing career comes first, then the chances of having a stable, intimate relationship with another person may be minimized, though certainly not ruled out. In my own case, in 1970 I made a decision to remain an artist-teacher rather than pursue the professional career I was offered in Germany. At the time I was concerned whether my voice could hold up in a strenuous operatic career, but an overriding concern was maintaining a stable lifestyle for my family. My early career as an artist-teacher proved plenty stressful, but at least I was at home most of the time. Now I wish I'd been able to give even more quality time to my family, especially to our three young sons. Again, I'm reminded that too soon we get old, and too late we get smart.

Many singers sustain active professional careers and enduring relationships with their life partners, though sacrifices may be required. Mezzo-soprano Stephanie Blythe speaks eloquently about the benefits of having a "significant other":

> I have to come back to what I said about all of life and art being interconnected. You can't just concentrate on singing and be a truly great artist. If you don't live, you have nothing to sing about. People are always worried about how their private lives are going to affect a career. It seems just the opposite to me. Since I've been married I think that my interpretation of a song like the Chausson "Sérénade" is much deeper. (Kubiak 2002)

Another lifestyle decision is the question of whether or not to have children. For instance, those who marry late and want children may face questions about pregnancy in older mothers. Once children are on the scene, parents need to find ways to give care and attention, including the necessities of living and as much TLC as possible. Many singers maintain healthy long-distance relationships by coordinating professional trips with educational and recreational travel for the family. Also, when away from home they stay in frequent contact via telephone calls, letters, and email.

In some cases, singers may sacrifice career objectives for the sake of the family. For instance, in the year 2000 Welsh bass-baritone Bryn Terfel canceled four months of high-profile singing engagements in order to be at home to assist with his wife's difficult pregnancy and the delivery of their third child. He proudly insists, "Singing isn't the be-all and end-all. I have other things in life and singing has to fit around those things now, whereas before life had to fit around my career" (Moss 2000).

It was my personal good fortune to marry at a young age and have three sons before age 26, a rare occurrence among young adults nowadays. The typical pattern among upwardly mobile professionals is to postpone marriage and children until the late 20s to early 30s, or even later. I certainly do not regret the fact that my wife and I had an early start. We now enjoy three uncommonly fine daughters-in-law and three wonderful grandchildren. In the long run, my family will undoubtedly rank among my greatest accomplishments, and I honestly feel family life has strengthened and balanced my professional life.

In making a decision about marriage and family, I again urge the young singer to keep in mind long-term goals and aspirations. For instance, what do you want your life to be like following a potential professional singing career? In your later years, do you want to live mostly alone, supported chiefly by friends and distant relatives, or do you also want to have immediate family members around for love, companionship, and support? Be very careful in making a decision whether or not to marry — and especially what to do regarding children. Though I highly recommend marriage and family, I certainly do not advocate it for everyone, for many persons are not cut out to be spouses or parents.

I'm simply suggesting that you give the big picture serious thought at the outset of your career.

In addition to spouse and children, other loved ones in the singer's life also need attention, including parents, grandparents, other relatives and friends. Occasional telephone calls, visits, and letters may suffice. As email becomes more widespread, it's becoming easier to keep in touch. A singer's support network is extremely vital in maintaining a sense of belonging and roots, so it is incumbent upon the singer to create ways of staying connected and involved in the lives of relatives and friends.

A former doctoral student who became an artist-teacher at a reputable Midwestern college endured a two-year separation from her husband, who was pursuing his doctorate at a distant university. She explained that they survived the separation by communicating every day, mostly by telephone at a pre-arranged time. Using this approach, they felt almost as connected as when they were together, which was every few weeks when they would set aside weekends and holidays to be with each other. With email being so inexpensive, it seems possible for anyone now to maintain contact with loved ones on a regular basis.

Coping Strategies

Now that caregiving objectives of singers have been identified, what strategies that balance personal and professional goals can be used to achieve these objectives? What follows are some suggestions based partly on the publication, *First Things First* (Covey, Merrill, & Merrill, 1994), in which four principal lifestyle guidelines are proposed — *to live, to love, to learn,* and *to leave a legacy*.

To Live
First, essential needs — food, shelter, clothing, freedom,

and safety — must be met to form a solid foundation for good mind-body health. Of course, *needs*, which are not the same as *wants*, vary widely from person to person. Struggling singers are well advised to live within their financial means, rather than incurring debt from large student loans or unnecessary luxury-item purchases.

My wife and I have always shared a mutual commitment to a modest lifestyle, and over the past several years we've increasingly been reminded what an enormous burden it can be to possess lots of things. Just take a moment to think about all the many things you own, and consider that every single item requires some attention and care, including storing, placing, cleaning, maintaining, and moving from time to time. Modern life is complicated and stressful partly because we bring pain on ourselves by spending the bulk of our time and energy reacting to urgent things rather than creating important things.

So, when Bettye and I periodically take inventory of our possessions, the result has been to rid our home of clutter–the type of stuff that's never used and has little monetary or sentimental value. At the same time, we realize our stated goal of cutting back on possessions can be emotionally difficult, especially when it involves a decision to get rid of prized items. If I have any practical suggestion to a young singer it's this: live a modest lifestyle, carefully avoiding the accumulation of things you don't really need, and giving more attention to the people, projects, and activities that truly matter in your life.

To live well also means prioritizing. A strategic place to begin is to imagine what people might say about us at our eventual memorial service. What would we wish them to say? That we were a wonderful singer but a lousy human being? Hardly. For this reason, a recommended first step in determining a purpose and direction for your life is to write a personal mission statement that's based on time-tested principles and summarizes how you wish to live.

To live fully also involves focusing on the present and the process of daily living, rather than dwelling on past or future actions. Whereas the elderly frequently reflect on the past, most upwardly mobile professionals look to the future. Sadly, we often fail to live fully "in the moment", constantly engaging and interacting with our immediate environment. Focusing clearly and intently on one's current activity and environment requires "centering", a psycho-emotional state characterized by a calm mind and a sense of inner peace, which may be achieved through meditation. The meditative condition of "flow" is the result of intense involvement in a pleasurable activity, when time appears to move either faster or slower than normal.

In a *Classical Singer* interview (January 2000), world-renowned stage director Fabrizio Melano advises: "Stay centered as much as possible and don't get distracted by all the craziness going on around you. That requires doing work on yourself. We all have to find our center in everything we do and not just as singers but as human beings."

To Love
True self-esteem is earned through personal development and achievement, and therefore does not happen automatically. A deep sense of self-worth and self-respect gives us a foundation for loving others. Here, love, in its broader context and meaning, is referred to as the intentional desire and capacity to give attention, care, and psycho-emotional support to persons with whom one is affiliated — family, friends, colleagues, and "significant others".

Family relationships — parents, siblings, partners, spouses, and children — can be extremely important in providing a secure and comfortable home base. However, family relationships can also contribute to stress, especially when family members are not supportive of the singer's chosen profession. In any case, singers need to invest quality time and energy in developing and sustaining strong family ties, particularly in relationships with spouses, partners and young children, those who often feel most neglected because of the singer's irregular, nomadic lifestyle.

For singers who have few close family members, friends and colleagues can provide viable emotional support. These relationships also need care, possibly through email, letters, telephone calls, outings, and other time together.

In sum, singers need to cultivate and maintain close ties with life-affirming people who give energy rather than take it, whether they are family, friends, or colleagues. We also need to let these people know how important they are to us, and that they are appreciated for who they are, not merely for the things they do for us.

To Learn
Learning is a lifelong process that involves making continuous adjustments in our belief systems and behavior. At the root of all learning lies an innate desire to seek the *truth* (*reality*) of all life experiences. A person's ability to perceive the truth may be blocked by self-centered greed or pride or jealous interpretations of others. The highest form of humanity lies in transcending our egocentrism to accomplish a greater or ultimate good. As we grow to incorporate a broader universal-view, our perspective of who and what we are broadens and deepens, ultimately helping us become better-motivated learners.

In becoming well-rounded performers, singers need to

explore and develop the principal learning modes — auditory, visual, kinesthetic, and analytical. Most singers seem content to rely on a single predominant mode, unconsciously sabotaging their potential growth and chances for success.

Effective learning also requires a mindset more inclined toward *process* than *product*. For instance, if one fails to enjoy the complex processes involved in both singing and living, such crucial goals as performing well or living a good life may not be fully realized. In short, because the journey is equally as important as the destination in any life adventure, why not enjoy the scenery and unique experiences along the way?

Living fully in the present results in a *flow* experience, when one is completely absorbed in pleasurable activity. Hence, whether rehearsing, performing, or carrying on a conversation with another person, the ability to give full attention at any given moment usually results in the flow state.

To Leave a Legacy
Remember the memorial service concept discussed earlier? In preparation for leading what will be remembered as a well-balanced life, we need to answer at least three essential questions:

- As determined by my most cherished values or priorities, what is my life's mission (goals and objectives)?

- What am I doing (or need to do) to fulfill my life's mission?

- What legacy do I wish to leave the world upon my death?

To answer the above questions, begin by writing a mission statement, including references to the important principles, values, and qualities that will guide your life. Here's a template based on my own mission statement:

I wish . . .

- to live morally, ethically and purposefully, in accordance with natural laws, societal guidelines, and common sense;

- to seek beauty, truth, and understanding through continual self-development;

- to cooperate and collaborate with fellow human beings in creating a stimulating, just, and healthy living environment that enables all creatures to fulfill their innate life-potential;

- to lead a simple yet quality lifestyle focused on priorities and supported by modest consumerism;

- to organize activities around well-defined goals, with specific plans for accomplishing desired results;

- to establish and maintain a balanced relationship between work, rest, and recreation;

- to stay "centered" and passionately involved in the present, rather than dwelling unduly on past or future events;

- to accept the paradoxes and challenges of life with patience, grace, and courage; and

- to take constructive action to improve the quality of life for self and others.

Notice that, though the singer's life is centered on vocal performance, there is no specific mention about a vocal music career in my mission statement. Why? Probably because our occupations actually provide minimal information about who we are as human beings. Notice there is no mention of wanting to be a very successful classical singer, or achieving great fame. That's because when we identify what's truly important, singing is secondary to our whole-life experience, which is determined more by principles and values.

Based on our mission statements, the legacy each of us leaves is a composite of our entire life's activities, which includes our work but also extends far beyond it to encompass our personal lives. As singers, we hope to have made contributions to peoples' lives by touching them with our expressive artistry, by sharing our expertise, and by collaborating with colleagues in performing great music. As human beings, we hope to leave a legacy — of love, good will, and professional contributions — that has profoundly affected the lives of all whom we have known, including loved ones, friends, colleagues, and the general public.

Notable Quotes: The Singer as Caregiver

Is it possible to have a family, to be married, or to have a "significant other" while maintaining a singing career?

> Ramón Vargas has a very loving family life. His website includes photos of family at home around the table and the Christmas tree. There is a snapshot with his parents at their home in Mexico City — they are smiling proudly with their accomplished son.
>
> Dawn Upshaw told a reporter for the New York Times that she scrubs the bathrooms in her house in Westchester, New York, where she lives with

her husband and two kids. "Oh, yeah. I still do lots of scrubbing. I don't think of myself as some sort of queen," she said. . . ."We have a very ordinary household. The children, especially, bring everything into perspective. When I am on the road it is really, really hard. I find myself after about a week to ten days questioning myself: 'What AM I doing? Why AM I away from my children?' And what this does is make me really look at my calendar and not be afraid to say no. I am thankful that I have them." — Jamie James

I am married to another singer [more than 18 years], someone who understands just how dedicated you must be and the incredible demands such a career places on an artist. There is no question that sacrifices have to be made by both of us, and ground rules laid down. For example, we try never to be separated for more than four weeks at a time. We make efforts to join each other even if it means flying across the ocean to catch the other one's performance. And we put no restrictions on telephone calls, speaking often four and five times a day even internationally. We strive to be incredibly "adult" in shoving petty jealousies and confinements aside. We take great pride in each other's successes, most often more so than in our own. We strive always to see the big picture ahead of daily needs and wants. We see ourselves as being in it for the long run, and attempt to live our lives in a way that fulfills that dream. We have our failings, just like anyone else, but the bottom line is that we love each other, respect each other's needs, and are the best of friends. — Jennifer Larmore

Chapter 19

The Singer as Citizen

The Singer as Citizen Advocate

In a way, all professionals are advocates for their discipline. An advocate in vocal music is one who espouses and defends the role of singing as a worthy discipline and significant art form in society, and espouses the benefits of singing in developing well-balanced, sensitive individuals. Singers are generally thought of as committed professionals who love what they do and proudly assert their enthusiasm to the public at large. As influential performers, singers are fortunate to have public forums in which they can declare their devotion to music and art. Many singers enthusiastically speak about their profession to others, from novice students in high school musicals to accomplished vocal artists performing with major opera companies.

For the vocal artist, advocacy also extends to the arts in general, and to other important aspects of life, such as personal, social, political, and environmental arenas, most of which are discussed in previous chapters or other sections of this chapter. In addition to serving as accomplished vocal artists, singers are capable of extending their influence through other means, such as public speaking and writing about their art. Along such lines, many singers are experimenting with song programs based on specific social, political, and environmental themes, and presenting them with scholarly program notes and spoken commentary. Programs that balance educational value and entertainment, or serious and humorous material, create interesting performance events. The objective should be to inform and engage the audience through active participation, for example, by using singer-audience dialogue and/or group singing. Any conscientious effort to connect with people serves as the highest form of advocacy on behalf of the vocal music profession.

The Singer as World Citizen

Beyond relationships with loved ones, singers are a part of an extended human family that includes neighbors and fellow citizens of a certain locale, region, and country. Increasingly, our interdependent human relationships are even extending to peoples in all countries. Sometimes we become so centered on our individual selves and our human species that we fail to recognize the true significance of humanity's place in the unfathomable stretches of time and space. So, as citizens of the world, we have certain responsibilities that need our attention, beginning at home.

In the wake of the terrorists' destruction of the World Trade Center on September 11, 2001, the civic sensibilities of moral folk worldwide were rekindled, especially in the U.S., where a renewed sense of civic duty was proudly displayed. Jolted by this single horrific disaster we have grown more aware of our commonalities as human beings, and less concerned with our differences. Along with the outpouring of positive responses by U.S. citizens in the weeks following the disaster, the arts community rose to the occasion, presenting concerts that paid tribute to those who lost their lives in the disaster.

In light of this renewed awareness of citizenship, what is the singer's role as citizen? More fundamentally, what or who is a citizen, what is citizenship, and what is meant by community? In broad terms, a *citizen* is an inhabitant of a city or town or a member of a country (native or naturalized), having rights and owing allegiance, and entitled to privileges and protection. *Citizenship*, then, is the state of being invested with the rights, privileges, and duties of a citizen, or one who is viewed as a valued member of a society or community. Finally, a *community* may be thought of as a social group of any size whose members reside in a specific locality, share government, and have a common cultural and historical heritage.

In his insightful book — *A World Waiting to Be Born* (1993), M. Scott Peck addresses the issue of community, suggesting four stages. The first stage — *pseudo-community* — is built on pretense and superficial relationships ruled by manners in an inauthentic, sterile, and unproductive manner. The second stage he labels *chaos*, a noisy win/lose process in which differences are fixed covertly according to simplistic organizational norms. In the third stage — *emptiness* — everyone works very hard trying to eliminate whatever stands between themselves and community, confessing individual prejudices, hidden grievances, fears, and hatreds in public — a courageous process that produces conflicting emotions from great relief to despondency. The fourth and final stage is *community*, which is often achieved suddenly and dramatically, initiated by someone making a poignant statement that triggers an outpouring by others. Next follows a peaceful silence that leads to a unison spirit, and action that leads to a genuine sense of community.

Following Peck's guidelines, it is easy to recognize the types of communities we've all been involved in at various times in our lives. Actually, it's rare to find ourselves immersed in a genuine community. Usually, we struggle with situations that more resemble the stages of pseudo-community, with forays into the stages of chaos and emptiness. I've witnessed all four stages over the last decade in the workplace, and I'm pleased a sense of community has been attained gradually, thanks principally to strong and inspiring executive leadership.

In practical terms, the typical U.S. citizen is associated with a variety of communities, including a local neighborhood, a town or city, a county, a state, a region, the country, the continent, and the world. In addition, the vocal artist may be associated with many communities, including vocal, musical, educational, arts, and hosts of others, depending on his or her interests and affiliations.

Finally, the singer is a citizen of the world, with responsibilities and obligations that require taking a world-view in all situations. More and more, we find ourselves intersecting and interacting on world levels as vocal artists, and thanks largely to increasing access to modern transportation and rapid communication via the internet, barriers are gradually breaking down in areas such as the arts, science, commerce, tourism, and education.

How does the model singer demonstrate good citizenship? Answering this question involves looking at several areas of life. In sum, the model singer demonstrates good citizenship by:

- cooperating and collaborating with neighbors to create a local neighborhood that is safe, attractive, and pleasant to live in;

- upholding democratic ideals, including participation in the political process and voting in all elections (for the singer, this includes participation in unions and organizations such as the American Guild of Musical Artists (AGMA) and the National Association of Teachers of Singing (NATS);

• protecting the environment through personal action (recycling, advocacy) and stewardship (lifestyle, financial support);

• abstaining from excessive consumerism and managing the use of material possessions wisely and economically;

• donating to worthwhile charities and organizations that demonstrate fiscal responsibility; and

• working with persons of all types of backgrounds, religions, and races to create a world based on tolerance and mutual respect.

The majority of singers are not wealthy (and most likely never will be), but Joseph Campbell's guidelines for using money wisely provide a poignant view of good citizenship. In his inspiring book — *Reflections on the Art of Living* (1991) — Campbell says: "Money experienced as life energy is indeed a meditation, and letting it flow out instead of hoarding it is a mode of participation in the lives of others."

As for my own role as citizen, I've tried to be a moral, ethical human being, abiding by society's laws and regulations as best as possible. Along with my family, I've also paid great attention to environmental concerns, beginning with recycling efforts in 1970 and modest annual donations to numerous environmental causes and organizations. In politics, I've made it a point over the past 20 years to vote in all major elections where important issues are at stake, but, like most singers, I can't claim to be a political activist. Indeed, I find it difficult to become enthusiastically involved in most political causes, though I occasionally write letters in support of preferred issues. Regardless of my inactivity in the political arena, I sincerely believe it's important for singers to take their citizenship and political heritage seriously, and contribute as much as possible in terms of time, effort and finances.

The Singer as Environmental Citizen

Sometimes we humans forget or ignore that we are composed of stardust, that we are part of all that has been, is, and will be. We are, figuratively, a minute speck in time, space, and nature. Nevertheless, we are inclined to think of ourselves as the highest form of creation and the masters of nature, endowed with the right to dominate and shape our natural environment to suit our every whim. While we should be proud of our species, a more realistic perspective of humankind might inspire us towards a deeper appreciation for the infinite magnitude, aesthetic features, structural order, and powerful forces of creation.

On the other hand, I believe one significant role we play as humans is our role in the world of nature, which we generally tend to take for granted. As a highly developed and civilized species, most humans are accustomed to all the modern conveniences, many of which serve to isolate us from the great outdoors. For example, in addition to providing us with shelter, protection, and comfort, our homes, buildings and vehicles also serve to insulate us from nature's many positive attributes.

Throughout my personal conversations and in reading written interviews featuring professional singers, I've noted that seldom is there any significant mention of the role nature plays in their lives. Though singers frequently mention the necessity of having close friends and loved ones, only occasionally does a singer mention the importance of taking a break from a heavy performing schedule to enjoy being outdoors for recreational or inspirational purposes.

It's amazing how hard we human beings work to shut ourselves off from nature, even though much of what we sing about concerns various aspects of nature — creatures, plants, land forms, and so on.

Think about it. How many singers can you name who are avid nature lovers? How many singers profess enthusiasm for spending time in the outdoors — walking, hiking, biking, camping, or sightseeing? It seems we're missing something vital, especially when we realize how many songs present texts describing a multitude of natural phenomena. For instance, there are probably as many songs about trees, flowers, birds, animals, mountains, fields, and forests as there are about people and their creative products. Inexplicably, many singers are unmoved by the powerful lessons to be learned from active participation in outdoor activities.

Gardening is a way close to home to connect with natural life processes. Though my wife and I have maintained small vegetable gardens in the past, we now do well to manage the lawn, shrubbery, flowers, and numerous trees and wild plants that adorn our home lot, which is connected at the rear to a marsh pond. Here, we are blessed with the daily and seasonal bliss of viewing a natural area containing a variety of wildlife including squirrels, ducks, geese, birds of all types (even an occasional hawk, owl, or egret), and sometimes muskrats, raccoons, woodchucks, and the like.

We also make it a point to periodically get outdoors beyond our immediate home environment to experience special natural areas. Some of our most enjoyable experiences have been mountain hikes in the Western United States and the Austrian Alps, and biking trips in Minnesota and Wisconsin. Though we've canoed a bit in the summer, in the summer of 2003 we enjoyed our first rafting adventure, which taught us about the awesome forces of rushing water and immobile rocks — and the welcome expertise of our whitewater rafting guide. Obviously, experiencing any of the above-mentioned natural phenomena first hand provides a more profound understanding that is communicated in the performance of songs that contain pertinent texts.

Alas, though nature provides salutary rest from the many stresses of modern life, nature is also under siege from humans — the most devastating species ever to inhabit this planet. The damage we inflict on our planet is legion: (1) noxious pollution of the air we breathe, the water we drink, and the land we inhabit; (2) destruction and/or depletion of natural resources, including irreplaceable water, energy sources, and valuable materials; (3) overbuilding and overuse of land, contributing to rapid depletion of farmland; (4) overcrowding of metropolitan areas caused primarily by increased and unchecked population growth; (5) indulgent consumerism and rampant growth based chiefly on economic concerns rather than basic human needs; (6) flagrant overuse and abuse of public lands by careless recreational users; and (7) special-interest political groups promoting personal and self-aggrandizing agendas.

Now that we have a clearer idea of the inspirational value of nature in our lives, as well as the problems we have created in the name of "progress", we must ask ourselves what role each of us can play in protecting and preserving our natural resources for posterity. There are two strategies we can use to deal with this issue, one to practice modest consumerism, and manage the use of material possessions wisely and economically; and the other to protect the environment through personal action (recycling, advocacy) and stewardship (lifestyle, financial support).

Though I mentioned earlier the need for singers to maintain a simple life style based on modest consumerism, the larger picture takes into account one's harmonious stewardship of all resources, natural and man-made. In theory and practice, the idea is this: the less we consume the more natural resources we save. Moreover, the less "stuff" we have to maintain and preserve, the more time we have to concentrate on the things that really matter. I'm constantly aware of the need to cut back and simplify, though I admit it's difficult to decide what needs to be recycled.

For many years my family has recycled all household materials that are collectible, beginning with our hauling containers of broken glass, cans, plastic, and cardboard to recycling centers, even though on at least one occasion a tire was punctured by debris scattered over the pickup area. We also recycle leftover food materials through composting, which can be a minor inconvenience in winter, when the Northland ground is frozen solid. (My solution is to chop everything up in a large plastic bucket using an ice chipper, place the bucket on the deck or dump it on the frozen compost pile — if the snow isn't too deep — and wait for the first spring thaw.)

Stewardship of resources also means caring for possessions and extending their life as long as possible. Though capitalism is a wonderful economic system, one of its shameful aspects is the concept of "planned obsolescence", which adds increasing tons of garbage to the world's overwhelmed landfills. There's not much that can be done to counter the need for the most up-to-date technology (who doesn't desire the fastest and most efficient computer possible?), but we could do a better job of re-engineering and reclaiming outdated technology equipment.

Our family's solution to acquiring possessions is to buy

used items, whenever possible, use them as long as possible, and care for them as best we can. For example, most of our cars have been driven at least 8-10 years, normally over 100,000 miles, and because they're mostly in top condition, our sons adopt and drive them a few more years. Currently, I'm driving an old Chevy Blazer inherited from my mother. It's a gas-guzzler, but in excellent condition with low mileage. Since I conscientiously maintain this car, I plan on driving it sparingly as a second vehicle for at least a few more years.

Each of us can do our part to protect the environment through advocacy and financial support of environmental organizations. Though my wife and I belong to several environmental groups, I must confess that our major support has been modest financial contributions, plus occasional letters to politicians in support of certain worthy causes. I've often thought of giving a special concert on Earth Day, perhaps based on poems about natural phenomena, of which there are many possibilities. Perhaps some reader will take the bait and undertake this worthwhile project in conjunction with a local environmental organization.

Finally, I hope this chapter has stimulated your thinking about the singer's life as a whole, and how daily choices fit into the big picture.

> *I sing, yet meaning more to me*
> *Are close friends and family,*
> *Loved ones all I hold so dear,*
> *My fellow beings, both far and near.*
> *Nature's all-embracing power*
> *Cradles us in life's brief hour;*
> *May we in our small valiant way*
> *Live with joy each glorious day.*

Notable Quotes: The Singer as Citizen

What is the relationship of your ethnic heritage to your status as an international singing star, and what does it mean to be a responsible world citizen?

> I do not just feel Mexican; I am proud of it, and I am also proud of representing Mexico worldwide. The fact that I am Mexican gives me confidence; I couldn't imagine myself having a different nationality. Though I obviously am a "citizen of the world", settled in Switzerland, my true identity is Mexican; I cannot and don't wish to change it, because of what I've lived through as a little boy and because of all the things my country gave me since my first years at the Basilica of Guadalupe, in the quarter of La Villa, the very heart of Mexico City. Thanks to these roots, I feel self-confident, authentic, unique. — Ramón Vargas

How do singers of color handle racial discrimination in our culture?

> I make a conscious choice to have a positive and healthy attitude. There are a lot of people controlling the whole thing and making the decisions. If you want to talk about racism, of course it exists in the world, because people are human beings. "Racist" is a difficult word for me, but I think we all have prejudices . . . When I walk through the door, I'm a black woman; there's no mistake about that. That's the first thing you see; that's who I am. . . I don't ever want to be in a position where I have to defend my blackness. I am who I am and I'm as committed and as passionate as anybody is in this business. My career is riding on my talent and passion and investment in myself as an artist. The audience is

sophisticated and I think they come to the theatre because they enjoy that art form. I know it's an issue for some people, but it's certainly not an issue for me.
— Denyce Graves

Chapter 20

The Singer as Achiever

Climbing the Mountain of Success

On May 29, 1953, 33-year-old Edmund Hillary from New Zealand was the first to reach the summit of Mount Everest, the world's highest mountain. Later, Hillary traveled to the South Pole and was the first to climb the highest peak in Antarctica. Hillary led the first jet boat expedition up the Ganges River in India to reach the river's source high in the Himalayas. Hillary also built schools, hospitals, and airfields for the Sherpa who lived in the vicinity of Mount Everest, and he produced three major books, including *High Adventure* (1955), an account of his Mount Everest climb.

Few of us will live life as adventurously and on the edge as Sir Edmund Hillary. Nor can most of us expect to reach the very top of the highest "mountain" in our profession as he did. On the other hand, like Edmund Hillary, who as a youth climbed the mountain peaks of his native New Zealand, young singers can improve their chances of succeeding when they chart a realistic course, take time to master the basics, maintain self-discipline, and adhere to the expectations of their chosen profession.

I don't profess to understand all of life's intricacies and mysteries, and certainly don't know all the ropes. Most of the advice I offer is common knowledge in the professional world of singing. Yet it helps to think about general guidelines periodically, somewhat like reviewing our New Year's resolutions with an eye to working toward the ideal, even if we fail to fully realize it.

A few years ago each member of the voice faculty at the University of Minnesota presented a brief talk at our weekly sessions for voice majors. My presentation focused on six steps for achieving success as a vocal student. I recommend that you consider each step, and write down any questions or thoughts that you have.

1. Identify Your Strengths, Resources, and Aspirations

Begin with a personal assessment. Answer the question: Who am I? Specifically, what are the personal characteristics that make me unique and special? What are my strengths and weaknesses, both as a person and as a vocal musician? What resources do I have at my disposal, including living situation, financial means, and educational tools? Am I pleased with my physical appearance? What are the positive aspects of my personality, and which areas need improving? As a vocal musician, how do I, and others, rate my level of talent and ability?

Are you aware of your primary motivations in life and your innermost desires? Are you self-directed or other-directed? One of the saddest observations I've experienced is students whose psycho-emotional states and life patterns are determined largely by fulfilling expectations set by other people, organizations, and institutions, rather than following the dictates of their own hearts. Until a belief and behavior system is one hundred percent your own, it cannot be truly effective. This is not to say that one should not adopt the beliefs and expectations of others, but only to emphasize the importance of claiming them as one's own.

I was fortunate to be surrounded by people who supported and encouraged my singing. The only cautious word I recall was my father voicing his concern about prospects for employment as a singer. Though he originally encouraged me to become a commercial artist, he never insisted on that pathway and his support of my vocal music interests was always firm. I was lucky in this regard, but I've known students who have had to go against the wishes of their parents to become singers, and it wasn't an easy process. In most cases, it pays to heed the advice of Joseph Campbell, with his encouraging words: "Follow your bliss".

2. Determine Your Principal Goals and Roles

What is your principal mission in life? What kind of person do you want to be? What roles will you play and how will you fulfill them? As mentioned earlier, when initiating a self-help program, Stephen Covey recommends "beginning with the end in mind". I particularly like his suggestion to imagine attending your own memorial service and listening to the eulogies offered by people associated with you over your lifetime.

Another obvious question is what kind of vocal musician do you wish to be? Can you be satisfied with achieving a moderate level of professional success, or do you expect to achieve an exceptional level of accomplishment? There's no right or wrong answer, but you must be willing to accept the consequences of your innermost desires and expectations. Becoming a major vocal artist carries a big price in terms of time, energy, and overall lifetime commitment.

Begin by making a list of objectives of two categories: personal and private. You may need some time to think about the things that are most important to achieve in your life, so don't feel rushed. Pay attention to your passions, as well as your realistic observations about yourself. Note anything that comes to mind at the outset, and later delete objectives that are unrealistic and unattainable.

3. Prioritize Your Objectives

Since you probably have lots of exciting objectives, it will help to order them in both personal and professional categories according to importance. By prioritizing your objectives, you will be guided in committing the requisite time and effort needed to reach the goals you deem most important. First list your top priorities, narrowing them down to four or five each in personal and professional categories.

To give you an idea of how you might prioritize your own goals, it might be helpful to see *my* top four priorities:

- *Mind-body Health.* This is my number one priority, which explains why I exercise first thing in the morning every day. Eating well, resting, and recreating are extremely important, as everything we do depends on the status of our overall health and level of mind-body energy.

- *Personality characteristics.* Being a well-rounded, positive-minded, optimistic, enthusiastic, receptive person is also a top priority; this is made easier if one feels well and healthy.

- *Social relationships.* Being a cooperative, collaborative team player is the next priority. This characteristic involves developing a strong emotional IQ, or the ability to empathize and communicate with others.

- *Learning, or the acquisition of essential knowledge and skills.* Being an enthusiastic, curious, receptive learner is extremely important, not only for developing coping skills, but also for the thrill of learning. Top learning priorities for singers include musicianship, vocalism (especially technique), linguistic expertise, and performance skills.

4. Develop a Realistic, Comprehensive Plan For Your Life

Do you have an overall rough-draft plan for your life, or are you playing it by ear, day by day? Does your plan include short-range, mid-range, and long-range goals? During high school and college, many goals are predetermined. For example, the typical college student is expected to fulfill prescribed institutional goals that include completing certain courses, numbers of credits, and accumulating respectable grade point averages. Though it's convenient to have preset goals, individuals need to set specific goals that include and complement formal study guidelines that form a major portion of the overall plan.

People vary in their ability to create effective "master plans" for their lives. For example, I've known students who set their sights on completing a masters degree in two years, and others who didn't appear to have any time-frame guidelines, just taking their time as they were swept along by the currents of circumstances and events. Even more incomprehensible to me are students who have spent years pursuing advanced degrees, have finished all requirements except for a final recital and/or paper, and simply drop out altogether. In some cases, students have reappeared years later, hoping to complete their degrees. Invariably, they are shocked to learn that it's more expensive, additional make-up work may be needed, and they have to re-audition for admission. Beware the perils of procrastination!

My experience as a graduate student may be helpful. At that time my professional schedule was very intense — including a college teaching position, two church choirs, professional singing engagements, and busy family life — so I had to be very efficient in time management. Therefore, at the outset I mapped out a four-year master plan that involved summer study, three annual recitals (each connected with research project papers), and a full year of residency. In preparation I learned everything I needed to know about the requirements, procedures, courses, credits, etc., and developed a master plan that I followed faithfully. Because of my initiative and follow-through, I could not but notice that I finished the degree much quicker than fellow doctoral students. Though there may be logical explanations for taking more time in completing one's goals, following a master plan can yield positive results.

Now let's consider *your* plans. Assuming successful completion of all academic studies, what do you want to happen following graduation? Will it be time to seek a teaching position, go for a performing career, or settle into a family life? It's an open book, isn't it? And that's what makes life exciting.

A mountain climb or a road trip into new territory is made more enjoyable if we have an accurate, detailed map for guidance. Lacking a good map, we might travel randomly, depending on our instincts and impulses to guide us. While this may be a wonderful way to enjoy a long hike or travel, it should not be adopted as a normal course of action. Contrary to the romantic notion that our lives are guided by fate, we actually have a great deal of control over our existence — especially in a culture where freedom of thought and action are encouraged and upheld.

5. Reassess Your Goals and Plans Periodically

Have some circumstances in your life changed: marriage, family, job, or health? If so, perhaps it's time for reassessment and revision of your goals and plans.

Although my own goals have undergone many changes over the course of my life, I've remained clearly focused on my life's mission. I started out as a child and adolescent visual artist, developed into a singer during high school, and in college majored first in philosophy, then music. My music career took a winding path, including service as a church musician, a high school choir director, part-time professional singer, voice teacher, choral director, opera director, pedagogy instructor, mid-level administrator, and, in recent years, author of vocal music textbooks. So, who says we can't reinvent ourselves along life's journey, changing our goals as we continue to learn and grow?

6. Follow Through With Accomplishing Your Goals

Finally, what approach do you use in accomplishing your goals? When each objective is completed, do you check it off on your "to do" list, and, when one is not completed, do you carry it forward for attention at some future date? In any case, the purpose is to follow through with your good intentions. Here are some guidelines for accomplishing your goals:

- *Understand your basic nature and your preferred approach to solving problems.* Do you budget enough time for completing all the goals you've set for yourself? Obviously, we cannot plan in advance everything we will do in our life, so we need to remain flexible and creative in dealing with changing opportunities and realities. All of us have individual approaches and responses to planned and unforeseen situations. For example, I consider myself a *concrete-random* type of person, which means I prefer a fairly structured and stable life, with specific objectives to be achieved flexibly within a certain time frame. So, though the courses I teach tend to be well organized and structured, I also like to allow some flexibility for assignments and class activities, with an attitude that "going with the flow" may sometimes be more productive than an activity I had planned in advance.

- *Work consistently at improving any weaknesses.* If you are principally a visual learner, work at developing your aural, kinesthetic, and analytical learning skills. If you are either more of a left-brain (analytical/classical) or a right-brain (intuitive/romantic) person, work at developing the opposite characteristics so as to enhance whole-brain activity. In general, singers and teachers need to integrate all learning/teaching modes to perform effectively as vocal musicians.

- *Strike a balance between your desired goals and realistic expectations of achieving success.* First, determine how much time and effort you need to accomplish your objectives, without becoming either overloaded or under-challenged. The idea is to set the stage for success by mastering all essential tasks in a timely and pleasurable manner. Though it may be hard to turn down certain opportunities, such as joining your friends for a trip or accepting yet another performance commitment, you must learn how to utter the liberating, time-freeing two-letter word, "NO", in conjunction with the one syllable word "THANKS" — without appearing resentful or apologetic. In short, realize your limitations, and live according to your personal life-code.

- *Maintain written records.* Everyone benefits from keeping a personal date-book or calendar into which all activities and tasks can be scheduled, including time for work, study, rest, recreation and, of course, vocal music activities. Rather than creating restraints, scheduling activities in advance actually frees you to pursue your most desirable goals. In conjunction with the date-book/calendar, you'll also need to maintain a "to do" list of daily, weekly, and monthly objectives. Though you may think it's possible to remember everything, don't trust your memory. Write *everything* down! Besides, scratching off tasks when completed provides a great sense of accomplishment, especially for goal-oriented personality types.

Final Words of Advice

In this closing section, I'd like to share two inspirational guidelines to spur you on to greater achievement as a singer. I've often told my students that singing is not for wimps. Only the brave-hearted, courageous, and most committed souls make it into the Vocal Kingdom. With that caveat, here are my final words of advice:

- *Always bear in mind the three "Ps" of success: Practice, Persistence, and Patience.* When you've done your best to improve your singing through regular and persistent practice habits, be patient in allowing time for your hard work to accumulate, gestate, and propagate. Rather than giving in to quick fixes, commit yourself to finding more permanent solutions. Some singers are hare-like sprinters, always giving everything as they speed toward their goals. Other singers are tortoise-like marathon types, plodding slowly but steadily forward to reach their goals. Ideally, of course, singers need to combine sprinter and marathoner characteristics, integrating the best qualities of both hare and tortoise.

- *Finally, realize that a successful vocal journey is more the result of concentrating on process than on product.* In this age of quick-fixes and instant-gratification, we often settle for superficial results in the quest for excellence. But we will need to learn to enjoy the *process* when we consider that a vocal performance amounts to less than 10 percent of the total time, effort and energy required, while 90 percent is devoted to preparation.

In learning to appreciate and enjoy the entire learning process, including all of the tedious hours of study and practice, we gradually achieve a true understanding of accomplishment through mastery. George Leonard, a martial arts instructor and author of a small but powerful book entitled, *Mastery: The Keys to Success and Long-Term Fulfillment*, provides a few words of wisdom well worth heeding:

> We fail to realize that mastery is not about perfection. It's about a process, a journey. The master is one who stays on the path day after day, year after year. The master is one who is willing to try, and fail, and try again, for as long as he or she lives (Leonard, 1992).

Though we are challenged to master and fulfill many goals and roles as singers, with the dawning of each new day we are given a fresh chance to resume our self-exploration, self-discovery, and self-realization as singers. I sincerely wish you an exciting and rewarding vocal music career, and hope this book has been helpful to you. I leave you with the following thoughts:

> *May your wide-ranging thoughts and deeply felt emotions*
> *Be conveyed on freely flowing breath, tone, and words*
> *To the ears, minds, and hearts of receptive listeners;*
> *For the purpose of inspiring and motivating them, and yourself,*
> *In transcending the mundane routines of daily life,*
> *Uplifting common human experience to a higher awareness,*
> *Revealing what it means to be completely human, and truly alive,*
> *Encouraging full participation in the vibrant presence, and*
> *Thereby instilling an optimistic outlook for the years to come.*

Notable Quotes: The Singer as Achiever

How do the most successful singers motivate themselves across a lifetime?

> "At the beginning of my career, I never imagined I would arrive at the point where I am now. What I have accomplished is the result of determination and perseverance, of never losing sight of my goal; it is also the result of a certain inner harmony that pushes me to set new aims for myself without expecting instant gratification, but with the peace of mind one gets from hard work and effort applied to following a clearly-defined path . . . What really matters in Art, as in any other activity, is a constant effort towards a precise goal, with emotional as well as intellectual direction . . . A permanent disposition to learn is essential. At sixty-four, Gigli still wanted to learn, after a forty-year career!" — Ramón Vargas

How hard was it to rise from your Midwestern roots to a successful singing career?

> I was never the person who got singled out or told that I had what it takes to be a singer. I was as surprised as anybody else to achieve this success. It had more to do with ignorance and blind optimism than anything else. I didn't realize how difficult it could be to get started in the business. When I look back on it now I think, 'My God, I was really lucky.' It just never occurred to me that I wouldn't get to do what I wanted if I was willing to work hard enough. You know that Midwestern work ethic. — Jerry Hadley

What is your most powerful motivation as a singer?

> When you live only for the destination, your life will have long periods of waiting between destinations. But when you live for the path, your life will feel as though every moment is integrated and you are doing exactly what you want to be doing. — Derek Mithaug, The Juilliard School

Bibliography

Books

Alderson, Richard. *Complete Book of Voice Training*. West Nyack, NY: Parker Publishing, 1979.

Balk, H. Wesley. *The Complete Singing Actor*. Minneapolis, MN: University of Minnesota Press, 1977.

Balk, H. Wesley. *Performing Power*. Minneapolis, MN: University of Minnesota Press, 1985.

Barbe, Walter & Raymond Swassing. *Teaching through Modality Strengths*. Columbus: Zaner-Bloser, 1979.

Barzun, Jacques. *Begin Here: The Forgotten Conditions of Teaching and Learning*. Chicago: University of Chicago Press, 1992.

Blades-Zeller, Elizabeth. *Singing With Your Whole Self: The Feldenkreis Method and Voice*. Lanham, MA: Scarecrow, 2002

Brown, Oren L. *Discover Your Voice*. San Diego, CA: Singular Publishing Group, 1996.

Brown, William E. Vocal *Wisdom: Maxims of Giovanni Battista Lamperti*. Brown; Crescendo Press, 1973.

Bunch, Meribeth. *Dynamics of the Singing Voice*. New York-Wien: Springer-Verlag, 1995.

Caldwell, Robert. *The Performer Prepares*. Dallas, TX: Pst...Inc. (with supplementary video), 1990.

Caldwell, Timothy J. *Expressive Singing: Dalcroze Eurhythmics for Voice*. Prentice Hall: Englewood Cliffs, NJ, 1995.

Campbell, Don. *The Mozart Effect*. New York: Avon Books, 1997

Campbell, Joseph. *Reflections on the Art of Living*. New York: HarperCollins, 1991,

Covey, Stephen R. Merrill, A.R. & Merrill, R.R. *First Things First*. New York: Simon & Schuster, 1994.

Covey, Stephen R. *The Seven Habits of Highly Effective People*. New York: Simon & Schuster, 1989.

Doscher, Barbara. *The Functional Unity of The Singing Voice*. Metuchen, NJ: Scarecrow Press, 1994.

Emmons, Shirlee, & Thomas, Alma. *Power Performance for Singers: Transcending the Barriers*. New York: Oxford, 1998.

Fields, Alexander. *Training the Singing Voice*. New York: King's Crowns Press, 1947.

Frankl, Victor. *Man's Search for Meaning*. New York: Washington Square Press, Simon and Schuster, 1963.

Gardner, Howard. *Frames of Mind: The Theory of Multiple Intelligences*. New York: Basic Books, 1983.

Goleman, Daniel. *Emotional Intelligence*. New York: Bantam Doubleday Dell Publishing Group, 1995.

Goleman, Daniel. *Working With Emotional Intelligence*. New York: Bantam Books, 1999.

Highstein, Ellen. *Making Music in Looking Glass Land: A Guide to Survival and Business Skills for the Classical Musician*. New York: Concert Artists Guild, 1993.

Hillary, Edmund. *High Adventure: The 50th Anniversary of the Historic Climb.* New York: Oxford University Press, 2003.

Kemp, Anthony E. "Individual Differences in Musical Behavior". *The Social Psychology of Music* (eds. D.J. Hargreaves and A.C. North). New York: Oxford University Press, 1997.

Lazarus, Richard S. *Emotion and Adaptation.* New York: Oxford University Press, reprint 1994.

Lazarus, Richard S. & Folkman, Susan. *Stress, Appraisal, and Coping.* New York: Springer Publishing Co., 1984.

Leonard, George. *Mastery: The Keys to Success and Long-Term Fulfillment.* New York: Plume (Penguin Books), 1992.

Madaule, Paul. "The Tomatis Method for Singers and Musicians". *About the Tomatis Method*, eds. T. Gilmore, P. Madaule, & B. Thompson. Toronto: The Listening Centre Press, 1989.

Madaule, Paul. *When Listening Comes Alive.* Norval, Ontario: Moulin Press, 1994.

Maslow, Abraham H. *Motivation and Personality* (rev. ed.). New York: Harper & Row, 1970.

McKinney, James C. *The Diagnosis and Correction of Vocal Faults.* Nashville, TN: Genevox Music Group, 1994.

Miller, Richard. *National Schools of Singing: English, French, German, and Italian Techniques of Singing Revisited.* Lanham, Maryland: Rowan and Littlefield, 2002.

Miller, Richard. *On the Art of Singing.* New York: Oxford University Press, 1996.

Miller, Richard. *Solutions for Singers: Tools for Performers and Teachers.* New York: Oxford University Press, 2003.

Miller, Richard. *The Structure of Singing: System and Art in Vocal Technique.* New York: Schirmer Books, 1986.

Papolos, Janice. *The Performing Artist's Handbook.* Cincinnati, Ohio: Writer's Digest Books, 1988.

Peck, M. Scott. *A World Waiting to Be Born.* New York: Bantam Books, 1993.

Reid, Cornelius. *A Dictionary of Vocal Terminology: An Analysis.* New York: Joseph Patelson Music House, 1983.

Sataloff, Robert T. *Vocal Health and Pedagogy.* San Diego: Singular Press, 1998.

Seligman, Martin E. P. "Positive Psychology". *Handbook of Positive Psychology.* (eds. C. R. Snyder and S. J. Lopez). New York: Oxford, 2002

Slobada, John. *The Musical Mind: The Cognitive Psychology of Music.* New York: Oxford University Press, 1987.

Tomatis, Alfred. *The Conscious Ear.* Tarrytown, New York: Station Hill Press, 1991.

Tomatis, Alfred. *The Ear and Language.* Norval, Ontario: Moulin Publishing, 1996.

Vennard, William D. *Singing: The Mechanism and The Technic.* New York: Carl Fischer, 1967.

Ware, Clifton. *Adventures in Singing, Third Edition* (text/song anthology/CDs). New York: McGraw-Hill, 2004.

Ware, Clifton. *Basics of Vocal Pedagogy: The Foundations and Process of Singing.* New York: McGraw-Hill, 1998.

Ware, Clifton. Voice *Explorations: The Bad, the Good, and the "Other".* Demo CD. 2003.

Weber, Ann L. *Introduction to Psychology.* New York: HarperCollins, 1991.

Willett, Walter C. *Eat, Drink, and Be Healthy.* New York: Simon & Shuster, 2001.

Wormhoudt, Pearl S. *With a Song in My Psyche: On the Psychology of Singing and Teaching Singing.* Philadelphia: Xlibris, 2002.

Articles

Barnett, Connie. "Career Steps: Where Do I Go From Here". *Classical Singer.* June: 12,14,15,21, 2003.

Bernheimer, Martin. "The Thinking Man's Thinking Man" (Thomas Hampson). *Opera News.* January: 29-33, 2001.

Carbajal, Gil. "The Student Becomes a Master". *Classical Singer*, July: 8-12,25-27, 2003

Davis, Pamela. "Emotional Influences on Singing". *Australian Voice*, 4:13-18, 1998.

Edwin, Robert. "Five Decades of Observations and Applications". *The NATS Journal.* January/February: 35, 48. 1992.

Edwin, Robert. "The Winds of Change." *The NATS Journal*, 49, 3: 35, 1993.

Ellison, Cori. "Victorian Era" (Victoria De Los Angeles). *Opera News*, January: 12-14, 1995.

Gough, Marion M. "The Healing Power of Music". *Classical Singer*, October: 56-61, 2003.

Gregg, Jean W. "Hearing and Noise Pollution". *Journal of Singing.* 55,3: 69-72, 1999.

Günter, Freeman. "My Voice is a Way of Life" (Jennifer Larmore). *Classical Singer.* June: 9-12, 28-30, 2002.

Günter, Freeman. "On the Plateau" (Marcello Giordani), *Classical Singer*, Sept. 2001, p. 40)

Günter, Freeman. "Our Man for the Millennium" (Thomas Hampson). *Classical Singer*. January: 8-9,26, 2000.

Günter, Freeman. "The Thinking Man's Soprano". (Patricia Racette). *Classical Singer*. October: 9-11,32-33, 2001.

Heirich, J.R. "The Alexander Technique and Voice Pedagogy." *The NATS Journal*, 49, 5:16-18, 1993.

Helfgot, Daniel. "Connecting the Dots." (Joyce Didonato). *Classical Singer*, August: 9-11, 25-29, 2003.

Holmes, Leslie. (Interview with Dawn Upshaw). *Journal of Singing*, September/October 2000: 53)

Kubiak, David. "An Operatic American in Paris" (Alan Held). *Classical Singer*, November: 12-15,34, 2001.

Kubiak, David. "Blythe Spirit" (Stephanie Blythe). *Classical Singer*, October: 8-11, 46, 2002.

Lander, John. " What Role Does the Ear Play in Singing", *Australian Voice* (1996: 57-65)

Leeda, K.J. "American Diva" (Denyce Graves). *Classical Singer*, September:13-15, 2002.

Madaule, Paul. "Listening and Singing". *Journal of Singing*. 57, 5: 15-20, 2001.

Makridakis, Marney K. "Those Who Can, TEACH". *Classical Singer*. September: 26-29, 2002.

Meier, Peg. "Born to Make Music" (Agnes Lisowsky). *Minneapolis Star Tribune*, November 17, 2002.

Moss, Stephen. "Singing Isn't the Be-All and End-All". *The Guardian*. Manchester, UK. October 12, 2000.

Nockin, Maria. "A Singer's Best Friend". (Edoardo Müller). *Classical Singer*, October: 23-25, 68, 2003.

Necular, Cristina. "Now, All the World's His Stage" (Thomas Hampson). *Classical Singer*. October: 11-21, 62-63, 2003.

Necular, Cristina. "Ramón Vargas". *Classical Singer*. July: 8-9, 22-23, 29, 2002.

Necular, Cristina. "Vienna State Opera's Sculptor of Singers — Ioan Holender." *Classical Singer*, October: 26-28, 2003.

Sadler, Cindy. "Planning for Success". *Classical Singer*. May: 14-15, 26, 2003.

Sataloff, R.T. "Hearing Loss in Singers". *The NATS Journal*. January/February: 35-39, 1991.

Shelton, Laurie S. "Vocal Problem or Body Block? A Look at the Psyche of the Singer". *Journal of Singing*. May/June, 1997.

Spoto, Donald. "Flicka in 3/4 Time" (Fredrica von Stade). *Opera News*, 64, 9:24-30, 2000

Staropoli, B. "If You Encounter a Great Teacher: Remembrances of Jan de Gaetani." *The NATS Journal*, 49, 2: 27-33, 1993.

Tibbetts, George R. "A Point of View". *IPPSVP Intelligencer*. Philadelphia: Institute for the Psychological and Pedagogical Study of Vocal Performance. October: 1-4, 2001.

Titze, Ingo. "A Modern-Day Vocologist", *Journal of Singing*, March/April: 39, 1998.

Zedda, Paolo. "Linguistic Variants and Their Effects on the Singing Voice". *Australian Voice*. 4: 65-69, 1998.

Zouves, Maria. "A Conversation with Mignon Dunn: An Intimate Rap Session". *Classical Singer.* January: 12-13, 34-35, 2001.

Zouves, Maria. "Fabrizio Melano, Part II". *Classical Singer.* January: 20-21, 2000.

Web Resources

Adventures in Singing:
　　http://www.mhhe.com/ais3

Classical Singer (magazine):
　　http://www.classicalsinger.com

National Association of Teachers of Singing:
　　http://www.nats.org

National Center for Voice and Speech:
　　http://www.ncvs.org/ncvs/

Opera America:
　　http://www.operaamerica.org/topten.htm

Voice Foundation:
　　http://www.voicefoundation.org

Index

accompanist 126, 130, 169, 189, 193-194, 196
achiever 5, 231, 233, 235, 237, 239, 241
acoustics 36, 110, 168-169, 171
actor 7, 107, 113, 116, 121-122, 124, 165, 201
actress 14, 116
actuator 85, 98
adduction 91, 92, 170
Adventures in Singing (Ware) 9, 87, 101, 102, 246, 250
advocate 219
aerotitis 66
aesthetics 190
agonists 15, 40
Alexander Technique 24, 167, 202, 248
amateur singer 135
Ameling, Elly 43
American Guild of Musical Artists (AGMA) 141, 179
American Institute of Musical Studies 107
antagonists 15, 40
anxiety 6, 30, 34, 127-128, 160, 206
appoggio 43
apprenticeship 138
arpeggio 94
art song 9, 31, 43, 78, 98, 108, 126, 140, 150

articulation 15, 40, 86, 90, 102-104, 110, 139, 160, 171
articulators 29, 63, 85-86, 88, 102-103, 199
artistic triumvirate 120
artistry 3, 25, 82, 97, 115, 117, 119, 121, 128, 155, 174-175, 191, 217
artist-teacher 161, 180, 209, 211
aspirate onset 90
athlete 13, 45-46, 88, 133
attitude 7, 19, 26, 31, 33, 55, 67, 138, 142, 157, 189, 229, 238
audiologist 165-166
auditions 149, 154, 179
aural processor 5, 57, 59, 61, 63, 65, 67
authentic voice 8
balance 10, 18, 38, 44, 51, 55, 63, 90-91, 114-116, 122, 124, 142, 161, 173-174, 211, 220, 238
Balk, Wesley 36, 121-122, 243
baritone 104, 105, 113, 125, 210
Bartoli, Cecilia 55
Basics of Vocal Pedagogy (Ware) 9, 87, 101, 246
bass 55, 105, 210
Bayo, Maria 96

behavior 7, 11-14, 22, 27, 29, 30-32, 45-46, 57, 124, 143, 171, 178, 181, 190, 214, 232
bel canto 10, 85, 185
biofeedback 127, 160
biomechanics 170
bleat 43
Blythe, Stephanie 163, 209, 248
body alignment 25, 40, 88, 202 (*see also* posture)
body language 22, 29, 95, 124, 139, 160
bone conduction 61, 63, 64, 173
brain-wave 25
breath control 88
breath energy 202
breath/tone release 92-93
breathing 4, 25, 27, 29, 40, 84, 86, 88, 90, 92-93, 98, 123-124, 199, 201 (*see also* respiration)
breathing exercises 88, 201
breath-tone 198
breathy phonation 41, 90
business manager 5, 147, 149, 151, 153, 155
Callas, Maria 14
cantare come si parla 173
career options 133
caregiver 5, 205, 207, 209, 211, 213, 215, 217
Carreras, Jose 104, 185
centering 124, 213
cerebral cortex 27
charisma 16, 111
chiaroscuro 15, 42, 84, 92, 139, 173
children 62, 100-101, 134, 142, 158, 207-211, 213-214, 218

choir 17, 74, 134, 136, 145, 158, 237
citizenship 221-224
classical music 7, 9, 140, 198
classical singer 72, 125-126, 138, 140-141, 217
Classical Singer magazine 138, 153
Cleveland, Thomas 167
cochlea 60, 61
cognitive therapy 127
collaboration 10, 32, 115, 168-170, 177, 189, 193
collaborator 5, 189, 191, 193, 195-196
colleague 7, 31, 72, 108, 113, 145, 177, 179, 184, 189
coloratura 14, 43, 94, 150
communication 4, 8, 32, 59, 61-63, 86, 97-98, 102-103, 111-112, 117-123, 127, 134, 138, 162, 171, 174, 177-178, 184, 189, 193, 195, 202, 222
communicator 117
competition 133, 150, 179, 192, 203, 206
composer 15, 44, 71, 78, 94, 95, 103, 107, 108, 111, 112, 114, 121, 142, 174, 175
conductor 32, 72, 99, 109, 118, 179, 193, 194, 207
conflicts 189, 191, 194
consonants 35, 42, 63, 86, 94, 101-103, 120
coordination 33, 40, 45, 77, 86, 91, 110, 112, 160
coping strategies 24, 128
copyright 126, 143
counter-tenor 150

creative artistry 117
crescendo 84
Dalcroze Eurythmics 77
De Los Angeles, Victoria 186, 247
decrescendo 44, 84
diaphragm 110, 169
diction 40, 84, 85, 101-106, 120, 139, 160, 194
diet 46-48, 118, 148
disorder 22, 30, 64, 65, 66, 73
Domingo, Plácido 72, 185, 203
dramatic skills 8, 127, 174
dramatic speech 172
dramatic tenor 82
dramatic voice types 150
dualism 36-38
dynamic expression 94
dynamics 13, 23, 32, 43, 84, 94, 111, 118, 120, 139, 191, 194
dysphonia 171
ear, anatomy of 60
ear-training 75, 205
eating disorders 46
emotion 7, 15, 29, 80
emotional intelligence 23, 28, 32, 193
emotionalism 115
emotions 6, 7, 13-15, 25-26, 29, 31, 33-34, 81, 87, 98, 103, 111-112, 122, 124, 194, 198, 221, 240
employment 156, 158, 161, 179-180, 184, 206-207, 233
energizing 122
energy 7, 28, 38, 45-46, 50-52, 59, 79, 103, 122-124, 127, 163, 173, 197-199, 202, 212, 214, 223, 226, 233-234, 240

ensembles 33, 79, 189, 190, 192, 205
enunciation 102
ethics 126, 177, 190
eustachian tube 60
exercises 49, 50, 64, 77, 87, 88, 90, 91, 102, 199, 201
exhalation 40, 88, 91
expression 3, 4, 6, 8, 9, 14, 22, 25, 33, 63, 81, 87, 94, 95, 102, 106, 110-112, 114, 116, 121, 123, 128, 139, 144, 161, 169, 171-172, 174-175
Fach 82, 139
facial expression 25, 33, 95
falsetto 91
family 82, 100, 134, 137, 141, 145, 150, 152, 159, 162, 183-186, 209-210, 213-214, 217, 220, 223, 227-228, 236-237
feedback 7, 57, 61, 63, 64, 84, 110, 154, 155, 161, 164, 167, 206
Feldenkreis 167, 202, 243
fight-or-flight 25-26, 127
financial support 223, 226, 228
Fischer-Dieskau, Dietrich 104
fitness 46, 52, 53
Fleming, Renée 43, 44, 80, 96, 106, 163, 185, 207
flow experience 215
folk songs 9, 78
foreign languages 99-102
frequencies 59, 198
gastric reflux 47

gatekeeper 144, 179
gesture of inhalation 41, 93
gestures 25, 33, 87, 95, 100, 124, 139, 191
glissandi 91
glottal onset 90
goals 8-10, 6, 16-17, 24, 31, 33, 45, 50, 87, 109-110, 147-148, 152, 162, 182, 192-193, 195, 210-211, 215-216, 234-240
golden mean 37
Graves, Denyce 54, 129, 175, 203, 230, 248
Hadley, Jerry 68, 116, 186, 241
Hampson, Thomas 19, 20, 44, 67, 113, 125, 129, 145, 247, 248, 249
harmonic structure 77
healing 197-199, 203
health 5, 14, 17, 21, 23, 40, 45-47, 50, 67, 83, 96, 138, 141, 149, 160, 168, 197-198, 200-201, 203, 211, 234, 237
hearing loss 58-59, 64-67
hearing mechanism 61
high notes 129, 185, 200
humming 64, 87
imagery 27, 28, 87
inhalation 40-41, 88, 91, 93, 199
intelligence 5, 23, 28, 32, 138, 191, 193
intensity 35, 200
International Phonetic Alphabet (IPA) 94, 105
interpersonal relationships 32, 189, 192, 193-144
interpretation 6, 61, 94, 102, 109-112, 118, 121, 161, 174, 191, 194, 209

jaw 29, 40, 85, 86, 87, 92, 94, 98, 102, 199
jawing 103
jazz 72
Journal of Singing (JOS) 166, 168, 247, 248, 249
Knudsen, Arvid 7, 10
Lamperti, G. B. 43, 243
language 22, 29, 62, 95, 97-105, 111, 117, 119, 124, 126, 139, 160, 172
language proficiency 99
Larmore, Jennifer 33, 34, 130, 145, 164, 196, 218, 247
laryngitis 166, 171
larynx 4, 63, 85, 90, 98, 110, 169
Lawrence, Cynthia 54
learning modes 190, 214
left-brain 174, 238
legato 44, 78, 84, 94
liberal arts 19, 138
lieder 31, 43, 112, 129
lifecycle 225
linguistic expertise 100, 235
linguistic variants 104, 249
lip-buzz 87, 92
lips 40, 85, 86, 87, 94, 98, 102, 123, 199
listening 44, 58, 62-64, 67, 99, 101, 113, 128, 155, 195, 200, 207, 233
lyric soprano 144
lyric tenor 82
Madaule, Paul 62, 173
mannerisms 12, 13, 22, 191
marcato 78, 94
marketing 140, 152
mask 87, 92, 93
meditation 38, 127, 213, 223

Melano, Fabrizio 213, 250
memorization 76
mentor 7, 154, 180-185, 196
messa di voce 44, 94
mezzo-soprano 14, 33, 139
Miller, Richard 10, 112
mind-body connection 21
mind-body strategies 201
mission statement 16-17, 148, 213, 215-216
Misslin, Patricia 163
mnemonic strategies 27
model singer 179, 222
Mozart effect 140, 197, 244
muscle tension 199
musicality 123
musicianship 71-73, 76-80, 117, 119, 126-127, 155, 235
National Association of Teachers of Singing (NATS) 168, 223, 247, 248, 249
non-classical music 7
nutrition 46, 48, 50, 55, 88
onset 41, 90, 91
opera 10, 14, 17, 31, 33, 41, 42, 43, 45, 46, 72, 78, 80, 82, 85, 98, 99, 102, 103, 106, 107, 109, 113, 118, 126, 136, 138, 140, 141, 143, 144, 149, 150, 151, 153, 154, 158, 172, 173, 189, 200, 201, 219, 237
Opera News 54, 113, 207, 247, 249
opposites 15, 35-44, 115, 122
oratorio 33, 98, 140, 150, 153, 172, 173
passage zones 91
Pavarotti, Luciano 43, 72, 76, 78, 104, 108, 119, 200

pedagogue 10, 43, 159, 163, 168
pedagogy 17, 36, 43, 67, 137, 159-162, 168, 237
perceptual modes 190
performance anxiety 127-128, 160
performance skills 16, 81, 111, 147, 153, 160, 161, 235
persona 6, 16, 111
pharynx 110, 169
philosophy of singing 3, 11, 18
phonation 15, 40-41, 84, 86, 90-91, 110, 160, 201
phoneme 111
phrasing 94, 111, 120, 123, 129, 139
pitch 39, 43, 64, 72, 76-78, 84, 91, 94, 105, 123, 139, 170, 199, 200
pollution 57, 58, 59, 226
polyps 171
popular music 9, 14, 179
portamento 78
posture 5, 29, 63-64, 95-96, 124 (*see also* body alignment)
pressed phonation 41, 90
Price, Leontyne 185
professional singer 17, 136-138, 142, 145, 159, 161, 208, 237
pronunciation 95, 99, 102, 104-106, 120, 139
psycho-emotional issues 21, 154
psychology 21, 31, 36, 160
publicity 140, 152, 196

Quasthoff, Thomas 105, 164, 203
Racette, Patricia 113, 248
Ramey, Samuel 55
registers 15, 42, 84, 91
registration 42-43, 91, 160
Reid, Cornelius 8, 81
relaxation techniques 127
repertoire 14, 29, 36, 51, 78, 82, 98, 99, 105, 108, 118, 121, 125, 126, 128, 138, 140, 150, 153, 160, 161, 174, 185, 190, 193
resonation 15, 40-41, 86, 110, 160
resonator 85, 86, 98
respiration 15, 40, 86, 110, 160 (*see also* breath *and* breathing)
rhythm 39, 63, 76-78, 94, 119-120, 123, 139, 191
right-brain 175, 238
role model 142, 184
roles 7-10, 15, 45, 72, 74, 82, 99, 109, 113, 146, 150, 154, 167, 183, 186, 233, 240
scholarship 108-116
Schubert, Franz 9, 10
self-promotion 152
semi-professional 133-136, 206
sight-reading 73, 77, 78, 118, 205
singer-actor 7, 121, 122, 124
siren 91, 92
soft palate 92, 94, 98
solfeggio 77
soprano 14, 31, 33, 113, 135, 139, 144, 200, 207, 209
Sprechgesang 120, 172
Sprechstimme 120
staccato 78, 94
stage fright 34, 127
stage presence 16, 111
stress 14, 26-28, 30, 45, 50, 51, 118, 127, 214
stretching 48, 50, 88, 201
style 78
syntax 97
Tai Chi 24, 50
talent 3, 11, 16, 23, 28, 33, 71, 83, 87, 95, 114, 128, 133-134, 136, 147-148, 155, 163, 229, 232
teacher 7, 13, 17, 21, 68, 74, 82, 96, 112, 158-165, 167, 170-172, 179-184, 193, 209, 211, 237
teaching 10, 6, 8, 12, 17, 36, 73, 76, 82, 83, 103, 105, 135, 136-137, 151, 156, 157-164, 168, 180-184, 236, 238
technician 81
technique 9, 11-13, 15, 23, 25, 41, 43, 53, 54, 77, 81-85, 95-96, 115, 119, 121, 127-128, 135, 139, 161, 169, 170, 174-175, 198, 200-202, 235
tempi 94, 118, 120, 191, 194
tempo 23, 78, 139
tenor 72, 82, 104, 107, 108, 113, 119, 135, 150, 185, 200
Terfel, Bryn 43, 210
tessitura 51, 84
text 3, 16, 27, 43, 80, 87, 102-103, 106, 111, 117, 119, 121, 246

textual source 15, 94-95, 142, 174
throat 4, 14, 29, 41, 44, 53, 60, 62, 86, 92, 98, 103, 166, 173, 175, 176, 200
timbre 10, 23, 39, 41, 84, 128, 198, 199
time management 236
tinnitus 58, 65, 66
Titze, Ingo 165-167, 249
Tomatis, Alfred 61-64, 198, 245, 246
tone deafness 64
tone placement 92
tone quality 41, 63, 92, 117, 119, 173, 190
tongue 13, 29, 40, 85-87, 92, 94, 98, 102, 178, 199
tympanic membrane 60, 61
Upshaw, Dawn 105, 115, 143, 196, 217, 248
Vargas, Ramón 113, 217, 229, 249
Vennard, William 36
vestibular apparatus 60
vibrations 61, 64, 92, 197, 199, 200, 202
vibrato 43, 84, 94
vitamins 48, 53
vocal anatomy 85-87, 137, 169-70
vocal artist 143, 219, 222, 233
vocal athlete 45, 46, 88
vocal competitions 154
vocal ecology 8
vocal effect 43, 197
vocal efficiency 81
vocal folds 41, 63, 85, 90, 91, 92

vocal habit 151
vocal health 96, 160, 168
vocal instrument 8, 8, 13, 45, 51, 52, 110, 137
vocal mechanism 43, 90, 93, 98, 110, 112, 167, 202
vocal performance 3, 7, 8, 33, 39, 103, 109, 111, 117, 120, 136, 157-160, 169, 174, 192, 205, 216, 240
vocal potential 12, 134
vocal problems 11, 175
vocal process 15, 21, 40, 86, 87, 110, 160
vocal skills 83
vocal study 5, 76, 161
vocal tract 4, 14, 29, 41, 63, 66, 84-93, 173, 199
vocology 165-170
voice levels 172-173
voice production 10, 12, 14, 62, 64, 110, 171, 173
voice scientist 165-170
voice teacher 7, 13, 17, 74, 96, 158-159, 163, 165, 170, 179, 193, 237
voice type(s) 30, 51, 91, 126. 139, 150
Voigt, Deborah 55
volition 15, 40, 62, 86
von Stade, Frederica 143
vowels 35, 42, 63, 86, 90, 92, 94, 101, 102, 119, 120
warm-ups 49, 54
whistle/flute 91
wobble 43
word treatment 120
yin-yang 38
yoga 24, 27, 127, 199

To order additional copies
of this volume, please write to:

**Birch Grove Publishing
PO Box 131327
Roseville, MN 55113**

For faster service, please email us:
sales@birchgrovepublishing.com

Visit us on the web:
www.birchgrovepublishing.com